8 Florida FAST Grade 5 Math Practice Tests

Seven practice tests woven into one calm routine

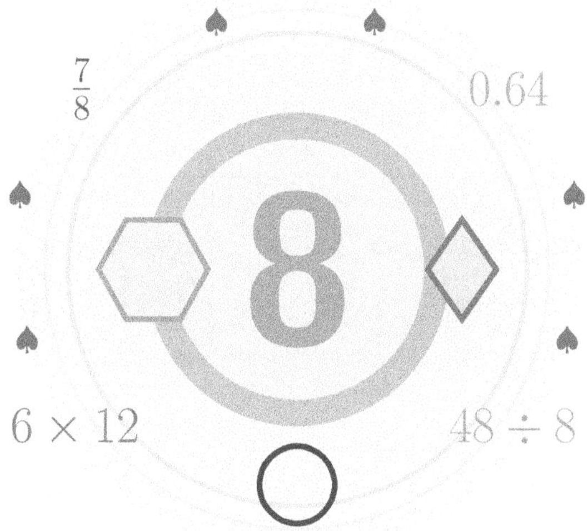

Eight full tests, a focused quick review, and helpful support that turns Grade 5 practice in The Sunshine State into steady, confident growth from page one to the final check.

Jay Daie and Reza Nazari

Copyright ©

Testinar Inc

Published by Testinar Inc

Testinar.com

Hello, Florida – Eight Tests, Steady Growth

Seven chances to read carefully, solve smartly, and grow stronger

To Florida Students Who Love a Puzzle

This practice book is your steady companion for eight tests, not a place to be perfect. Strong math work moves like a manatee in clear water: slow, steady, and full of quiet power.

Use these eight tests like stepping-stones. Take one test at a time, check your answers honestly, and notice which skills need more attention. Small improvements add up across seven rounds.

Read

Read every word twice and underline what is asked.

Solve

Choose the cleanest method and show your steps.

Reflect

Look back to find what worked and what to fix.

A strong habit for Florida mathematicians: read carefully, estimate when it helps, show your steps, and keep going even when a question feels tricky. That is how steady math confidence is built.

How This Book Wants to Help

A simple routine that turns practice into progress

Step 1: Power Up

Sharpen your math brain with the quick review.

Spend a few minutes waking up your memory before the test begins.

Step 2: Trail Run

Take a full practice test in a quiet spot.

Work in a calm spot and focus on careful thinking before speed.

Step 3: Debrief

Score honestly and circle missed questions.

Circle missed questions and notice which topics keep showing up.

Step 4: Repair

Fix the missed work and lock the lesson in.

Read the explanation, repair the work, and bring that lesson into the next test.

A Good 8-Week Florida Rhythm

Week 1	Take Test 1 like a clear morning paddle.
Week 2	Take Test 2 and slow down on word problems.
Week 3	Take Test 3 and lift fraction and decimal work.
Week 4	Take Test 4 and pay close attention to labels and units.
Week 5	Take Test 5 and compare your habits with your first test.
Week 6	Take Test 6 and practice staying calm during tricky questions.
Week 7	Take Test 7 with sunshine focus and careful checking.
Week 8	Take Test 8 and finish the journey with calm, careful, confident work.

Inside the Seven Practice Tests

What these eight practice tests help students build

These three practice tests prepare Grade 5 students in the Sunshine State for the bright, focused thinking the Florida FAST rewards. The goal is bigger than only getting answers right. Students are practicing how to read closely, choose a strategy, solve carefully, and explain their work when needed.

Selected-Response Questions

Students solve the problem and choose the best answer. Estimating first and crossing out weak choices can save time and points.

Constructed-Response Questions

Students show their thinking, steps, models, or explanations. Even when unsure, writing what they know can help organize the problem.

Grade 5 Skills You Will Practice Often

- place value, comparing numbers, and rounding
- multi-digit addition, subtraction, multiplication, and division
- fractions, decimals, and mixed numbers
- perimeter, area, volume, and measurement conversions
- coordinate points, patterns, graphs, and tables
- geometry and multi-step word problems

What strong work looks like on the FAST: the answer is correct, the steps are clear, the labels or units are included, and the final result makes sense.

Trail-Day Strategy Lab

Smart moves for calm, careful problem solving

Notice → Plan → Work → Recheck

Trail Setup

- square up your paper and set your pencil
- scan the directions like a checklist
- promise: careful first, fast later

Trail Run

- circle key numbers and key words
- estimate to check the answer's range
- leave a clean trail of your steps

Trail Reset

- draw a picture if the problem is wordy
- rule out answer choices that obviously do not fit
- save it for later – a calm look often unlocks it

Trail Wrap

- check labels: feet, dollars, minutes, etc.
- reread the question one final time
- ask, Does this answer make sense in real life?

A calm reset for the FAST: When the heat of test day rises, breathe like an Everglades morning: long and full of fresh air.

Steady Confidence

Confidence grows when Florida students practice, reflect, and keep going

Trade the Panic Voice for a Coach Voice

Instead of thinking...	Try telling yourself...
I am bad at math.	I am still building this skill.
This problem is impossible.	Let me find one small step I can take.
I will never finish in time.	Let me start the next small piece.
I missed it again.	Mistakes are how I learn what to fix.

Confidence Builders

- track scores and small wins
- notice one thing that improved today
- fix mistakes instead of hiding from them

A The Sunshine State Truth

Sunshine does not fight the rain. It just shows up again the next day, even brighter.

A powerful promise for this book: I will slow down, show my work, learn from corrections, and let practice make me stronger across all eight tests.

Watch Your Climb

A simple way to notice growth across all eight Florida tests

How to Use This Page

After each test, write your score, one topic that felt strong, and one next step. Track your score like the tide – gentle daily changes shape a long shoreline.

Test	Score	Best Move	What to Practice Next
Test 1			
Test 2			
Test 3			
Test 4			
Test 5			
Test 6			
Test 7			
Test 8			

A smart reflection question: Did my score change because I knew more math, checked my work better, or stayed calmer? Sometimes the answer is all three.

Pre-Test Tune-Up

Fast habits that warm up your brain before the real problem solving begins

Before the First Question

- read the directions all the way through
- look over the page without rushing
- begin with a clear pencil and an even clearer plan

While You Work

- underline what the problem really wants
- estimate when it helps you spot mistakes
- keep your work organized enough to easily check

Before You Turn It In

- check labels, units, and decimal points
- reread your final answer one more time
- make sure the answer truly fits the question

If Pressure Shows Up

- pause and take one slow breath
- solve only the next smallest part
- remember that one hard problem does not decide the whole test

A Florida truth for the FAST: being ready does not mean feeling perfect. It means feeling prepared enough to think clearly and to keep going.

Math Topic Compass

A simple map of the big Grade 5 math ideas tested on the FAST

Why This Page Helps

Grade 5 math feels much easier to review when Florida students know which skill family a question belongs to. Once they can name the family, they can focus practice in the right place instead of guessing what to study next.

Number Sense

Place value, decimals, fractions, and comparison

Operations

Multi-step computation, patterns, and reasoning

Measurement and Geometry

Area, volume, graphs, shapes, and coordinates

A useful review move: when you miss a question, do not stop at "wrong." Ask which skill family it came from. That single question points you straight toward the smartest next round of practice.

Grade 5 Skill Snapshot

Big domains and the kind of work students are expected to do

Domain	Focus Skills
Operations and Algebraic Thinking	Describe numerical patterns, compare how terms change, and reason about relationships in a rule or sequence.
Number and Operations in Base Ten	Use place value understanding and perform operations with whole numbers and decimals.
Number and Operations with Fractions	Compare fractions, find equivalent fractions, add and subtract fractions with like denominators, and multiply a fraction by a whole number.
Measurement and Data	Convert units, interpret line plots, and solve problems involving perimeter, area, and volume.
Geometry	Plot points on the coordinate plane and classify two-dimensional figures by their properties.

Study tip: if one domain feels shaky, spend extra time there before the next test instead of trying to review everything at once.

Family Practice Guide

Support for Florida families that feels calm, useful, and realistic

What This Book Is Designed to Do

This book gives Grade 5 students eight opportunities to practice Florida math in a real test-style setting and then learn from what happened. Sunshine practice is short and warm: a little focus daily beats a long burst once a week. The biggest gains usually come from short routines, honest review, and encouragement that feels steady rather than stressful.

What Is the FAST?

FAST stands for **F**lorida **A**ssessment of **S**tudent **T**hinking. It is given to Grade 5 students across Florida to measure progress on important math standards.

What Helps Most

- praise effort, patience, and clear work
- keep sessions short, regular, and predictable
- ask what your child learned from a mistake
- review missed problems without blame

What Gets in the Way

- turning practice into punishment
- rushing through hard problems just to finish
- comparing one child's score to another's
- focusing only on the final number

Quick Review Before Test Day

A short Grade 5 refresher for Florida students before you practice

Place Value and Rounding

- In 348,726, the digit 8 is in the thousands place, so its value is 8,000.
- Expanded form: 348,726 = 300,000 + 40,000 + 8,000 + 700 + 20 + 6
- To round to a place value, look at the digit to the right of that place.
- Example: 62,849 rounded to the nearest thousand is 63,000.

Order of Operations

Use this order:

1. parentheses
2. multiplication and division from left to right
3. addition and subtraction from left to right

$$18-2\times(3+4) = 18-2\times7 = 18-14 = 4$$

A Florida Word Problem

An orange grove has 36 rows with 28 trees per row. How many trees total?

Show your work clearly. Estimate first if it helps. Check labels and units before circling a final answer.

Helpful reminder: line up place values when adding or subtracting large numbers and decimals. Straight columns make checking much easier.

Fractions and Decimals

Fraction Facts

- numerator = how many equal parts you have
- denominator = how many equal parts make one whole
- equivalent fractions name the same amount

$$\frac{2}{3} = \frac{4}{6} = \frac{8}{12}$$

Add and Subtract Fractions

When denominators match, work with the numerators.

$$\frac{5}{8} + \frac{2}{8} = \frac{7}{8}$$

$$\frac{9}{10} - \frac{4}{10} = \frac{5}{10} = \frac{1}{2}$$

Multiply a Fraction by a Whole Number

$$4 \times \frac{3}{5} = \frac{12}{5} = 2\frac{2}{5}$$

This is repeated addition:

$$\frac{3}{5} + \frac{3}{5} + \frac{3}{5} + \frac{3}{5}$$

Decimal Place Value

In 3.472, the 3 is in the ones place, the 4 is in the tenths, the 7 is in the hundredths, and the 2 is in the thousandths.

$$0.5 = \frac{1}{2} \qquad 0.25 = \frac{1}{4} \qquad 0.6 = \frac{3}{5}$$

Compare carefully: with like denominators, compare numerators. With decimals, compare the whole-number part first, then tenths, then hundredths, then thousandths.

Measurement and Geometry

Perimeter, Area, and Volume

Perimeter is the distance around a figure.

$$P = 2l + 2w$$

Area measures the space inside a rectangle.

$$A = l \times w$$

Volume measures the space inside a rectangular prism.

$$V = l \times w \times h$$

If $l = 10$, $w = 3$, and $h = 4$, then $P = 26$ units, $A = 30$ square units, $V = 120$ cubic units.

Angles and Lines

- right angle = exactly 90°
- acute angle = less than 90°
- obtuse angle = more than 90° and less than 180°
- parallel lines never meet
- perpendicular lines meet at a right angle

A point on the coordinate plane is written as (x, y). For example, $(2, 5)$ means 2 across and 5 up.

Units matter: length uses units like inches or centimeters, area uses square units, and volume uses cubic units.

Data and Problem Solving

Numerical Patterns

Look for what changes each time.

3, 7, 11, 15

This pattern adds 4 each step.

4, 8, 16, 32

This pattern multiplies by 2 each step.

Tables and Graphs

- read the title and labels first
- check the scale before comparing values
- line plots often show fractions
- tables can reveal patterns and rules

A Strong Plan for Word Problems

1. Read the problem twice.
2. Decide what you need to find.
3. Choose the operation, model, table, or pattern that fits best.
4. Solve step by step.
5. Check with an estimate or with the opposite operation when possible.

Final reminder for Florida mathematicians: a quick review is not a race. It is a reset that helps you walk into the test ready to think clearly.

Florida Grade 5 Math Standards Reference

This rewritten guide presents the Grade 5 mathematics expectations for Florida, aligned to Florida B.E.S.T. Standards. The official standard code stays on the left; the explanation on the right restates the same expectation in new, classroom-friendly language.

MA.5.AR | Florida

This section focuses on grade 5 expectations grouped under MA.5.AR.

MA.5.AR.1	This standard asks students to solve problems involving the four operations with whole numbers and fractions.
MA.5.AR.1.1	The learning target is for students to solve multi-part real-life problems involving any combination of the four operations with whole numbers, including problems in which remainders must be interpreted within the context.
MA.5.AR.1.2	Students demonstrate understanding as they solve real-life problems involving the addition, subtraction or multiplication of fractions, including mixed numbers and fractions greater than 1.
MA.5.AR.1.3	Students should be able to solve real-life problems involving division of a unit fraction by a whole number and a whole number by a unit fraction.
MA.5.AR.2	This standard focuses on demonstrate an understanding of equality, the order of operations and equivalent numerical expressions.
MA.5.AR.2.1	This standard focuses on translate written real-world and mathematical descriptions into numerical expressions and numerical expressions into written mathematical descriptions.
MA.5.AR.2.2	Students demonstrate understanding as they evaluate multi-part numerical expressions using order of operations.
MA.5.AR.2.3	Students should be able to determine and explain whether an equation involving any of the four operations is true or false.
MA.5.AR.2.4	This standard focuses on given a mathematical or real-world context, write an equation involving any of the four operations to determine the unknown whole number with the unknown in any position.
MA.5.AR.3	This standard focuses on analyze patterns and relationships between inputs and outputs.
MA.5.AR.3.1	This standard focuses on given a numerical pattern, identify and write a rule that can describe the pattern as an expression.
MA.5.AR.3.2	This standard focuses on given a rule for a numerical pattern, use a two-column table to record the inputs and outputs.

MA.5.DP | Florida

This section focuses on grade 5 expectations grouped under MA.5.DP.

MA.5.DP.1	The learning target is for students to collect, represent and interpret data and find the mean, mode, median or range of a set of data.
MA.5.DP.1.1	Students demonstrate understanding as they collect and represent numerical data, including fractional and decimal values, using tables, line graphs or line plots.
MA.5.DP.1.2	Students should be able to interpret numerical data, with whole-number values, represented with tables or line plots by determining the mean, mode, median or range.

MA.5.FR | Florida

This section focuses on grade 5 expectations grouped under MA.5.FR.

MA.5.FR.1	The learning target is for students to interpret a fraction as an answer to a division problem.
MA.5.FR.1.1	This standard focuses on given a mathematical or real-world problem, represent the division of two whole numbers as a fraction.
MA.5.FR.2	This standard focuses on perform operations with fractions.
MA.5.FR.2.1	This standard asks students to add and subtract fractions with unlike denominators, including mixed numbers and fractions greater than 1, with procedural reliability.
MA.5.FR.2.2	This standard focuses on extend previous understanding of multiplication to multiply a fraction by a fraction, including mixed numbers and fractions greater than 1, with procedural reliability.
MA.5.FR.2.3	This standard focuses on when multiplying a given number by a fraction less than 1 or a fraction greater than 1, predict and explain the relative size of the product to the given number without calculating.
MA.5.FR.2.4	This standard focuses on extend previous understanding of division to explore the division of a unit fraction by a whole number and a whole number by a unit fraction.

MA.5.GR | Florida

This section focuses on grade 5 expectations grouped under MA.5.GR.

MA.5.GR.1	The learning target is for students to classify plane figures and three-dimensional figures based on defining attributes.
MA.5.GR.1.1	Students demonstrate understanding as they classify triangles or quadrilaterals into different categories based on shared defining attributes. Explain why a triangle or quadrilateral would or would not belong to a category.

MA.5.GR.1.2 Students should be able to identify and classify three-dimensional figures into categories based on their defining attributes. Figures are limited to right pyramids, right prisms, right circular cylinders, right circular cones and spheres.

MA.5.GR.2 This standard asks students to find the perimeter and area of rectangles with fractional or decimal side lengths.

MA.5.GR.2.1 The learning target is for students to find the perimeter and area of a rectangle with fractional or decimal side lengths using visual models and formulas.

MA.5.GR.3 Students demonstrate understanding as they solve problems involving the volume of right rectangular prisms.

MA.5.GR.3.1 This standard focuses on explore volume as an attribute of three-dimensional figures by packing them with unit cubes without gaps. Find the volume of a right rectangular prism with whole-number side lengths by counting unit cubes.

MA.5.GR.3.2 This standard asks students to find the volume of a right rectangular prism with whole-number side lengths using a visual model and a formula.

MA.5.GR.3.3 The learning target is for students to solve real-life problems involving the volume of right rectangular prisms, including problems with an unknown edge length, with whole-number edge lengths using a visual model or a formula. Write an equation with a variable for the unknown to represent the problem.

MA.5.GR.4 Students demonstrate understanding as they plot points and represent problems on the coordinate grid.

MA.5.GR.4.1 Students should be able to identify the origin and axes in the coordinate system. Plot and label coordinate pairs in the first quadrant of the coordinate grid.

MA.5.GR.4.2 This standard asks students to represent mathematical and real-life problems by plotting points in the first quadrant of the coordinate grid and interpret coordinate values of points in the context of the situation.

MA.5.M | Florida

This section focuses on grade 5 expectations grouped under MA.5.M.

MA.5.M.1 Students demonstrate understanding as they convert measurement units to solve multi-part problems.

MA.5.M.1.1 Students should be able to solve multi-part real-life problems that involve converting measurement units to equivalent measurements within a single system of measurement.

MA.5.M.2 This standard asks students to solve problems involving money.

MA.5.M.2.1 The learning target is for students to solve multi-part real-life problems involving money using decimal notation.

MA.5.NSO | Florida

This section focuses on grade 5 expectations grouped under MA.5.NSO.

MA.5.NSO.1 This standard focuses on understand the place value of numbers with several digits with decimals to the thousandths place.

MA.5.NSO.1.1 This standard focuses on express how the value of a digit in a multi-digit number with decimals to the thousandths changes if the digit moves one or more places to the left or right.

MA.5.NSO.1.2 The learning target is for students to read and write numbers with several digits with decimals to the thousandths using standard form, word form and expanded form.

MA.5.NSO.1.3 This standard focuses on compose and decompose numbers with several digits with decimals to the thousandths in multiple ways using the values of the digits in each place. Demonstrate the compositions or decompositions using objects, drawings and expressions or equations.

MA.5.NSO.1.4 Students should be able to plot, order and compare numbers with several digits with decimals up to the thousandths.

MA.5.NSO.1.5 This standard asks students to round numbers with several digits with decimals to the thousandths to the nearest hundredth, tenth or whole number.

MA.5.NSO.2 The learning target is for students to add, subtract, multiply and divide numbers with several digits.

MA.5.NSO.2.1 Students demonstrate understanding as they multiply whole numbers with several digits including using a standard calculation algorithm with procedural fluency.

MA.5.NSO.2.2 Students should be able to divide whole numbers with several digits, up to five digits by two digits, including using a standard calculation algorithm with procedural fluency. Represent remainders as fractions.

MA.5.NSO.2.3 This standard asks students to add and subtract numbers with several digits with decimals to the thousandths, including using a standard calculation algorithm with procedural fluency.

MA.5.NSO.2.4 This standard focuses on explore the multiplication and division of numbers with several digits with decimals to the hundredths using estimation, rounding and place value.

MA.5.NSO.2.5 Students demonstrate understanding as they multiply and divide a multi-digit number with decimals to the tenths by one-tenth and one-hundredth with procedural reliability.

Table of Contents

Grade 5 Math

Grade 5 Mathematics

1

Questions: 40 **Duration:** No time limit

Calculator Policy: Calculators are not allowed

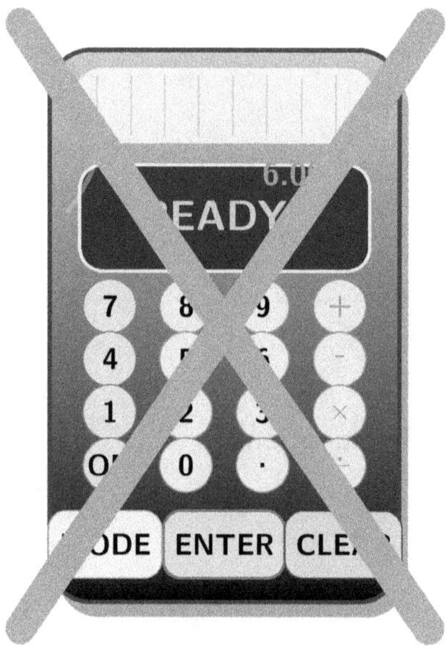

Grade 5 Mathematics Reference Materials

PERIMETER AND AREA

Perimeter of Rectangle	$P = 2l + 2w$ or $P = 2(l + w)$
Area of Rectangle	$A = l \times w$
Area of Triangle	$A = \frac{1}{2} \times b \times h$
Volume of Rectangular Prism	$V = l \times w \times h$

LENGTH

Customary	**Metric**
1 foot (ft) = 12 inches (in.)	1 meter (m) = 100 centimeters (cm)
1 yard (yd) = 3 feet (ft)	1 centimeter (cm) = 10 millimeters (mm)
1 yard (yd) = 36 inches (in.)	1 kilometer (km) = 1,000 meters (m)

CAPACITY

Customary	**Metric**
1 cup (c) = 8 fluid ounces (fl oz)	1 liter (L) = 1,000 milliliters (mL)
1 pint (pt) = 2 cups (c)	
1 quart (qt) = 2 pints (pt)	
1 gallon (gal) = 4 quarts (qt)	

WEIGHT AND MASS

Customary	**Metric**
1 pound (lb) = 16 ounces (oz)	1 kilogram (kg) = 1,000 grams (g)
	1 gram (g) = 1,000 milligrams (mg)

TIME

1 minute (min) = 60 seconds (sec)	1 week = 7 days
1 hour (hr) = 60 minutes (min)	1 year = 12 months
1 day = 24 hours (hr)	1 year = 52 weeks

1) A shape is a closed polygon with 5 straight sides and 5 vertices. Which statement correctly describes the shape?

☐ A. It is a pentagon.
☐ B. It is a quadrilateral.
☐ C. It must be a rectangle.
☐ D. It has curved sides.

2) Which calculation is FALSE?

☐ A. $0.95 \div 10 = 0.095$
☐ B. $37 \div 1000 = 0.037$
☐ C. $8.4 \div 10 = 8.4$
☐ D. $6.1 \div 100 = 0.061$

3) Two friends are cutting rope. One piece is $\frac{3}{5}$ meter and the other is $\frac{1}{4}$ meter. What is the total length?

☐ A. $\frac{4}{9}$ meter
☐ B. $\frac{17}{20}$ meter
☐ C. $\frac{3}{20}$ meter
☐ D. 1 meter

4)

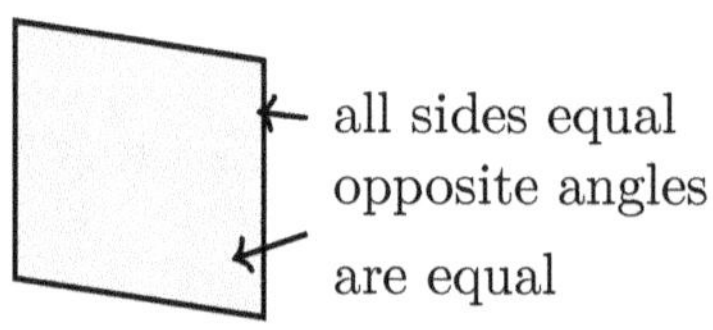

What is the BEST name for this figure?

☐ A. Parallelogram
☐ B. Rhombus
☐ C. Rectangle
☐ D. Trapezoid

5) A student wrote the ordered pair $(5,3)$ to describe a point that is 3 units right and 5 units up. What is the student's error?

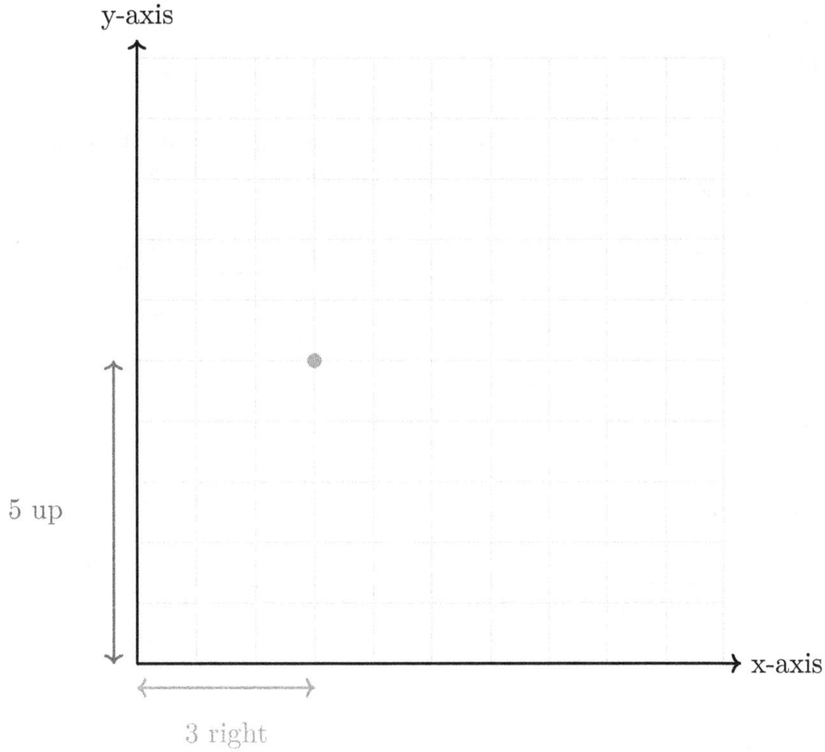

☐ A. The x-coordinate and y-coordinate are swapped

☐ B. Both coordinates are too large by 2

☐ C. The point should be $(3,3)$

☐ D. The axes are labeled incorrectly

6) An error was made. Student A says $\frac{1}{2} = \frac{2}{3}$. What is the mistake?

☐ A. Different denominators without equivalent form

☐ B. Denominators were added wrong

☐ C. Common denominator is wrong

☐ D. Numerators don't match

7) Mrs. Johnson earns \$18.50 per hour. If she works 20 hours per week, how much does she earn per week?

- ☐ A. \$350
- ☐ B. \$360
- ☐ C. \$370
- ☐ D. \$380

8) A water tank in the shape of a rectangular prism has dimensions 14 feet, 10 feet, and 8 feet. What is its volume?

- ☐ A. 280 cubic feet
- ☐ B. 840 cubic feet
- ☐ C. 1,120 cubic feet
- ☐ D. 1,400 cubic feet

9) Which expression evaluates to exactly 100?

- ☐ A. $(20 + 5) \times 4$
- ☐ B. $20 \times (5 + 4)$
- ☐ C. $(5 \times 5) + 4$
- ☐ D. $5 \times (25 - 4)$

10) A box has $V = 210$ ft^3, $l = 7$ ft, $w = 5$ ft. Find its height.

Record your answer in the space provided.

11) A library orders 105 boxes of books with 10 books per box. Total books?

- ☐ A. 105
- ☐ B. 1050
- ☐ C. 10500
- ☐ D. 115

12) Board A is $2\frac{1}{3}$ ft long, and Board B is $3\frac{2}{3}$ ft long. What is the total length of the two boards?

☐ A. $5\frac{1}{3}$ ft ☐ C. 6 ft
☐ B. $5\frac{2}{3}$ ft ☐ D. $6\frac{1}{3}$ ft

13) An area model can show $\frac{1}{2} \times \frac{1}{3}$. What is the product?

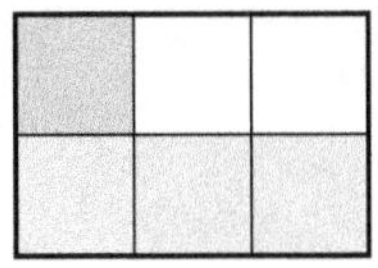

☐ A. $\frac{2}{3}$ ☐ C. $\frac{2}{5}$
☐ B. $\frac{1}{5}$ ☐ D. $\frac{1}{6}$

14) Two tape diagrams show expressions side-by-side. Which comparison is correct?

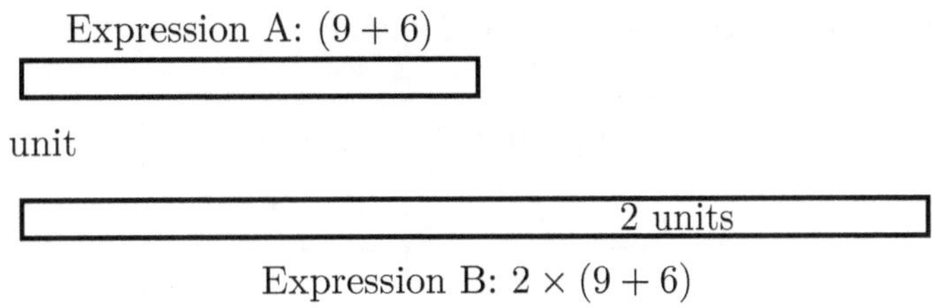

☐ A. A is 2 more than B ☐ C. A equals B
☐ B. A is 2 times B ☐ D. B is twice A

15) Pattern: the output is the input plus the same input again. Which statement is true?

☐ A. The output is double the input. ☐ C. The output is half of the input.
☐ B. The output is the input times itself. ☐ D. The output is 1 more than the input.

16) Divide: $735 \div 15$

☐ A. 47
☐ B. 49
☐ C. 51
☐ D. 53

17) How many cups are in 3 gallons? (Use: 1 gallon = 4 quarts, 1 quart = 2 pints, 1 pint = 2 cups)

☐ A. 12 cups
☐ B. 24 cups
☐ C. 36 cups
☐ D. 48 cups

18) Which statements describe triangles correctly? *Select all that apply.*

☐ A. A triangle has 3 sides.
☐ B. A triangle has 3 vertices.
☐ C. A triangle has 4 sides.
☐ D. A triangle must have a right angle.

19) Two number sequences are shown. Sequence 1: 5, 10, 15, 20, 25. Sequence 2: 1, 2, 3, 4, 5. Write the rule for Sequence 2 in terms of Sequence 1.

Sequence 1	Sequence 2
5	1
10	2
15	3
20	4

☐ A. Sequence 2 = Sequence 1 $\div 5$
☐ B. Sequence 2 = Sequence 1 -4
☐ C. Sequence 2 = Sequence 1 $\times 5$
☐ D. Sequence 2 = Sequence 1 $+1$

20) A small greenhouse model measures 12 meters long, 7 meters wide, and 2 meters tall. What is its volume?

☐ A. 84 cubic meters
☐ B. 24 cubic meters
☐ C. 14 cubic meters
☐ D. 168 cubic meters

21) A tailor needs $1\frac{3}{4}$ yards of fabric per shirt. She makes 8 shirts. How much fabric does she use?

☐ A. 15 yards
☐ B. 12 yards
☐ C. 13 yards
☐ D. 14 yards

22) Sam drinks $\frac{2}{3}$ of a $1\frac{1}{2}$-liter water bottle. How many liters does he drink?

Record your answer in the space provided.

23) Evaluate: $3 + 18 \div 6 - 1$

☐ A. 2
☐ B. 4
☐ C. 5
☐ D. 20

24) Find a fraction equivalent to $\dfrac{3}{4}$ with denominator 16.

Record your answer in the space provided.

25) Find: $\dfrac{1}{4} \div 2$.

Record your answer in the space provided.

26) How many zeros are in 10^6?

☐ A. 3 zeros
☐ B. 4 zeros
☐ C. 5 zeros
☐ D. 6 zeros

27) A warehouse ships $\frac{1}{4}$ of inventory one day, $\frac{1}{3}$ the next day. Remaining?

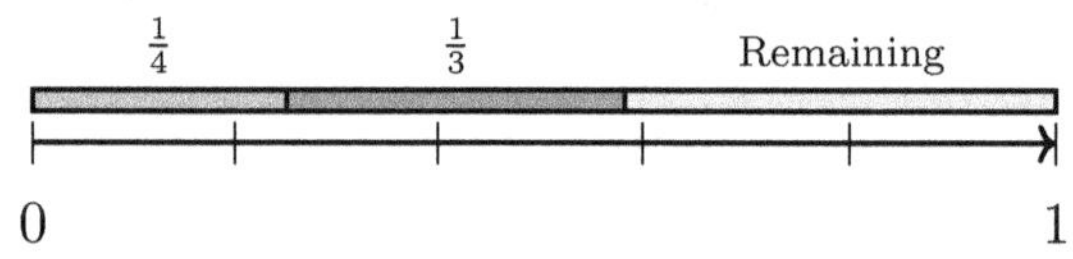

☐ A. $\frac{5}{12}$
☐ B. $\frac{7}{12}$
☐ C. $\frac{5}{7}$
☐ D. $\frac{11}{12}$

28) In a science experiment, the temperature rose by 0.6 degrees and later by 0.06 degrees. Which change was larger?

☐ A. The rise of 0.6 degrees
☐ B. The rise of 0.06 degrees
☐ C. They were equal
☐ D. Cannot compare

29) Which value equals 0.5 divided by 10,000?

☐ A. 0.05
☐ B. 0.0005
☐ C. 0.005
☐ D. 0.00005

30) Subtract: $\frac{7}{10} - \frac{1}{4}$

☐ A. $\frac{6}{10}$
☐ B. $\frac{6}{14}$
☐ C. $\frac{9}{20}$
☐ D. $\frac{13}{20}$

31) A student estimated $\frac{7}{15} + \frac{5}{13}$ and rounded both fractions to $\frac{1}{2}$, getting 1. Is this estimate within 0.5 of the true value?

- ☐ A. Yes, it is within 0.5
- ☐ B. No, it is too high
- ☐ C. No, it is too low
- ☐ D. Cannot tell without computing

32) A baker made 12.345 kg of dough. Break this number into its place values.

- ☐ A. $1 + 2 + 0.3 + 0.04 + 0.005$
- ☐ B. $12 + 0.3 + 0.04 + 0.005$
- ☐ C. $10 + 2 + 0.3 + 0.4 + 0.5$
- ☐ D. $12 + 3 + 4 + 5$

33) Round 4.5 to the nearest whole number.

- ☐ A. 4
- ☐ B. 4.5
- ☐ C. 5
- ☐ D. 6

34) Which expression represents "the difference of 25 and the product of 3 and 5"?

- ☐ A. $25 - 3 \times 5$
- ☐ B. $(25 - 3) \times 5$
- ☐ C. $3 \times (25 - 5)$
- ☐ D. $25 \times 3 - 5$

35) Maria buys 5 erasers at \$0.75 each. How much does she spend?

- ☐ A. \$3.25
- ☐ B. \$3.50
- ☐ C. \$3.75
- ☐ D. \$4.00

36)

20×10	5×10
20×3	5×3

$= 25 \times 13$

This area model shows 25×13 broken into four partial products. What is the total product?

- ☐ A. 315
- ☐ B. 325
- ☐ C. 335
- ☐ D. 345

37) A Venn diagram has a large circle for polygons. Inside it is a circle for quadrilaterals, and inside that is a circle for rectangles. Where should a geometric circle be placed?

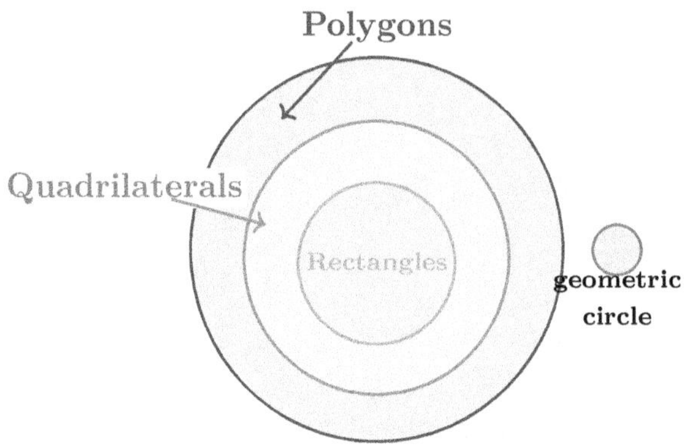

- ☐ A. Outside all three circles
- ☐ B. Inside rectangles
- ☐ C. Inside quadrilaterals only
- ☐ D. Inside polygons only

38) Rule A starts at 1 and adds 3. Rule B starts at 0 and adds 4. Which list gives the first four ordered pairs as (Rule A, Rule B)?

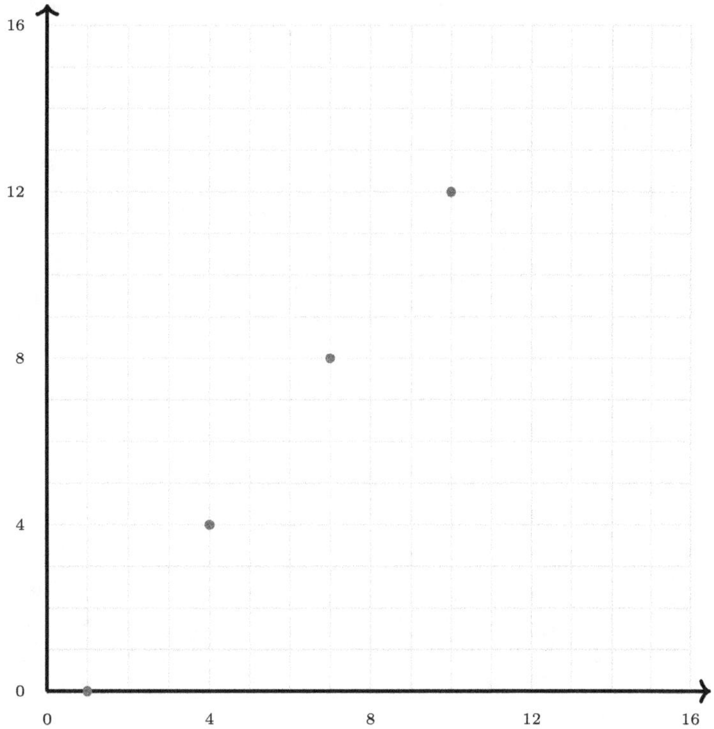

☐ A. (1,0), (4,4), (7,8), (10,12)

☐ B. (0,1), (4,4), (8,7), (12,10)

☐ C. (1,1), (4,4), (7,7), (10,10)

☐ D. (3,4), (6,8), (9,12), (12,16)

39) On a graph of distance traveled, the x-axis shows hours and the y-axis shows miles. A point is plotted at $(4, 20)$. How many miles does the point show?

Record your answer in the space provided.

40) Subtract: $8\frac{1}{3} - 2\frac{5}{6}$

- ☐ A. $5\frac{1}{2}$
- ☐ B. $5\frac{2}{3}$
- ☐ C. $6\frac{1}{2}$
- ☐ D. $6\frac{5}{6}$

End of Practice Test

Take a short breath, then check your work with care. Good corrections can teach almost as much as the test itself.

What-If Wizard! ✓

You finished a full test. That takes focus and stamina.
"What if?" is a magic phrase in math.

What If? Unlocks the Answer ★

Lucas loved asking "what if?" "What if I tried a smaller number first? What if I drew this differently? What if I worked backwards?"
Each "what if?" was a small experiment. Most failed, but each one taught him something. Eventually, one worked.
On 5th grade tests, when you're stuck, run a quick "what if" experiment. A wrong attempt teaches you what's right.

Math Mindset Tip: **Stuck? Try a what-if. Even a wrong attempt narrows the path.**

Every "what if?" is a step toward the answer.
— Math Mindset

Lucas's Amazing Journey ★

Lucas wasn't afraid to be wrong. He knew that being wrong on a tiny experiment was much cheaper than being wrong on the real problem.
Imagine you're stuck on a fraction problem. "What if I used $\frac{1}{2}$ instead of the actual fraction?" If you can solve the simpler one, the path is clearer.
Try Lucas's habit: when stuck, swap in friendlier numbers, solve the smaller version, and then return to the original.

Lucas's Secret: **Test your idea on a smaller problem first.**

Try this on your next practice test. Small, smart habits become big score boosters.

★ Ask "what if?" Then test it. ★

Brave guesses (with checking) lead to right answers.

Grade 5 Math

Grade 5 Mathematics

2

Questions: 40 **Duration:** No time limit

Calculator Policy: Calculators are not allowed

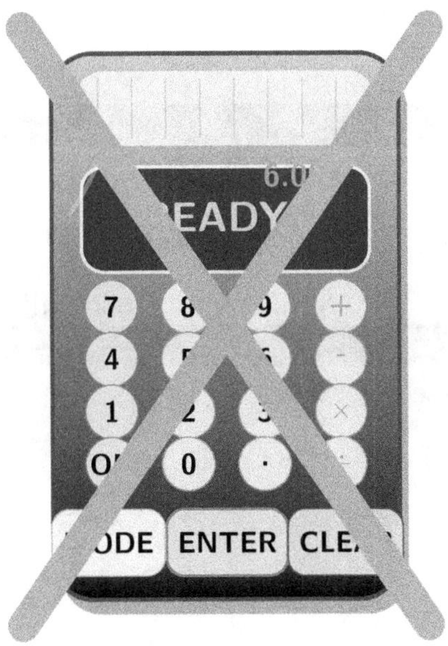

Grade 5 Mathematics Reference Materials

PERIMETER AND AREA

Perimeter of Rectangle	$P = 2l + 2w$ or $P = 2(l + w)$
Area of Rectangle	$A = l \times w$
Area of Triangle	$A = \frac{1}{2} \times b \times h$
Volume of Rectangular Prism	$V = l \times w \times h$

LENGTH

Customary	**Metric**
1 foot (ft) = 12 inches (in.)	1 meter (m) = 100 centimeters (cm)
1 yard (yd) = 3 feet (ft)	1 centimeter (cm) = 10 millimeters (mm)
1 yard (yd) = 36 inches (in.)	1 kilometer (km) = 1,000 meters (m)

CAPACITY

Customary	**Metric**
1 cup (c) = 8 fluid ounces (fl oz)	1 liter (L) = 1,000 milliliters (mL)
1 pint (pt) = 2 cups (c)	
1 quart (qt) = 2 pints (pt)	
1 gallon (gal) = 4 quarts (qt)	

WEIGHT AND MASS

Customary	**Metric**
1 pound (lb) = 16 ounces (oz)	1 kilogram (kg) = 1,000 grams (g)
	1 gram (g) = 1,000 milligrams (mg)

TIME

1 minute (min) = 60 seconds (sec)	1 week = 7 days
1 hour (hr) = 60 minutes (min)	1 year = 12 months
1 day = 24 hours (hr)	1 year = 52 weeks

1) A student wrote the expanded form of 9.452 as $9+0.4+0.005+0.002$. What error did the student make?

☐ A. This is the correct expanded form for 9.452.

☐ B. The hundredths term should be 0.05, not 0.005.

☐ C. The expanded form has five place values, but we can only use four.

☐ D. The student added fractions instead of decimal values.

2) Pattern: $3, 6, 11, 18, 27, \ldots$ The differences increase by 2 each time: add 3, then 5, then 7, then 9. What is next?

☐ A. 34

☐ B. 36

☐ C. 38

☐ D. 40

3) Show the division with a place-value arrow diagram:

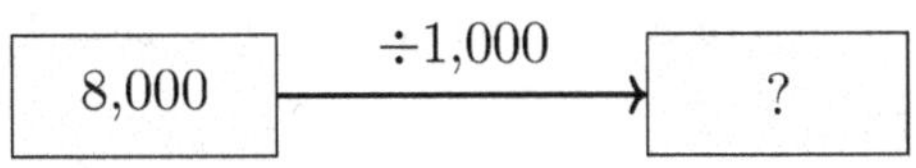

What is $8,000 \div 1,000$?

☐ A. 800

☐ B. 80

☐ C. 8

☐ D. 0.8

4) The table shows several products and their number of trailing zeros. Based on the pattern, how many zeros does 300×400 have?

Expression	Product	Zeros
3×4	12	0
30×40	1,200	2
300×40	12,000	3
300×400	?	?

☐ A. 4

☐ B. 5

☐ C. 6

☐ D. 7

5) A store sells rope in $\frac{1}{4}$-meter bundles. How many bundles are made from 9 meters?

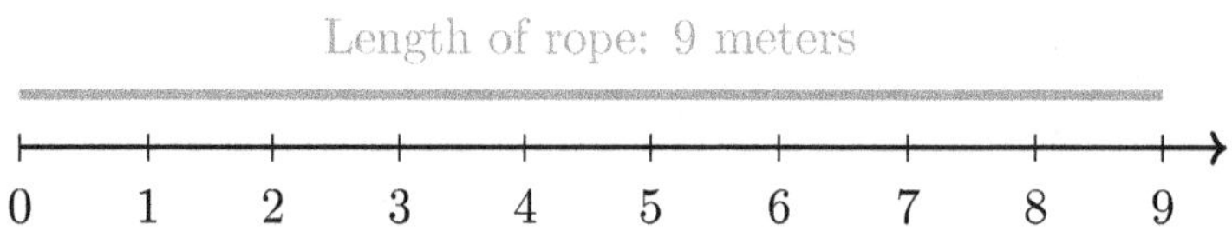

☐ A. 18
☐ B. 24
☐ C. 30
☐ D. 36

6) A rectangular prism has volume 540 cm^3, length 15 cm, and height 9 cm. What is the width?

☐ A. 3 cm
☐ B. 6 cm
☐ C. 5 cm
☐ D. 4 cm

7) A grocery store receives boxes of apples with weights: Box 1: 18.5 kg, Box 2: 21.75 kg, Box 3: 19.25 kg, Box 4: 18 kg.
If the shelves can hold 80 kg maximum, how much more weight can be added?

☐ A. 2.5 kg
☐ B. 5 kg
☐ C. 10 kg
☐ D. 12.5 kg

8) Write a division equation for: 5 cups of juice poured into $\frac{1}{4}$-cup servings.

Record your answer in the space provided.

9) On a coordinate plane, a quadrilateral ABCD has vertices at $A(1,1)$, $B(5,1)$, $C(5,5)$, and $D(1,5)$. What is the most specific name for this quadrilateral?

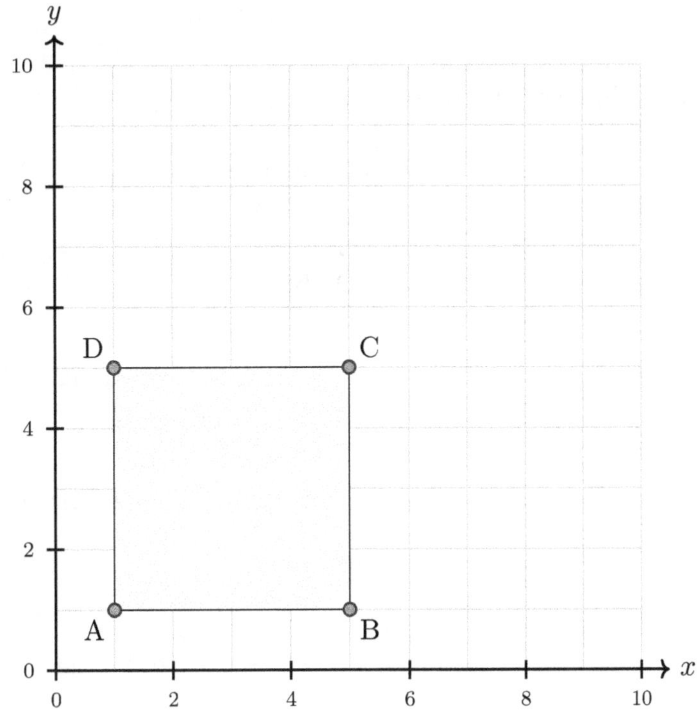

☐ A. Square
☐ B. Rectangle
☐ C. Trapezoid
☐ D. Parallelogram

10) Find: $9 \times \frac{2}{6}$.

Record your answer in the space provided.

11) Which measurement is smallest?

☐ A. 5,000 mm
☐ B. 50 m
☐ C. 0.5 km
☐ D. 600 cm

12) Which figure has volume as an attribute?

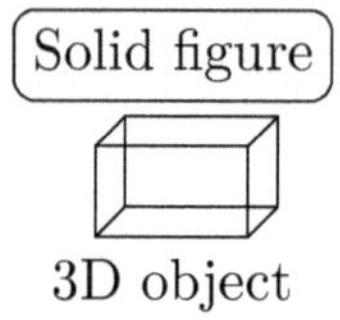

☐ A. A line segment
☐ B. A rectangle
☐ C. A rectangular prism
☐ D. A point

13) The line plot shows liquid measurements, in liters. What is the total amount of liquid shown?

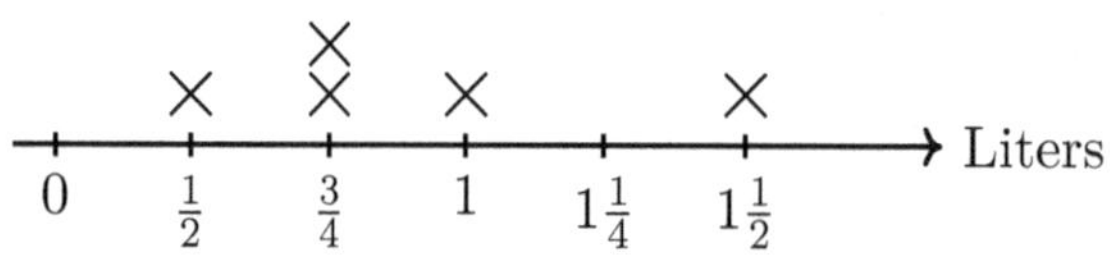

Record your answer in the space provided.

14) What digit is in the hundredths place in 4.06?

Record your answer in the space provided.

15) Which expression is greater: $(20 - 5) \times 3$ or $20 - (5 \times 3)$?

☐ A. $(20 - 5) \times 3$
☐ B. $20 - (5 \times 3)$
☐ C. The expressions are equal.
☐ D. Cannot be determined.

16) Which symbol makes this statement true? $7 \times \frac{2}{3}$ __ 7×1

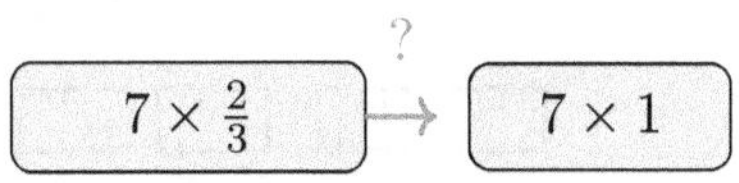

☐ A. Cannot determine
☐ B. =
☐ C. >
☐ D. <

17) A farmer divides land: $\frac{1}{3}$ for corn and $\frac{2}{5}$ for wheat. To compare, what common denominator should he use?

☐ A. 8
☐ B. 6
☐ C. 10
☐ D. 15

18) Use fraction circles. Which statement correctly describes the two pictures?

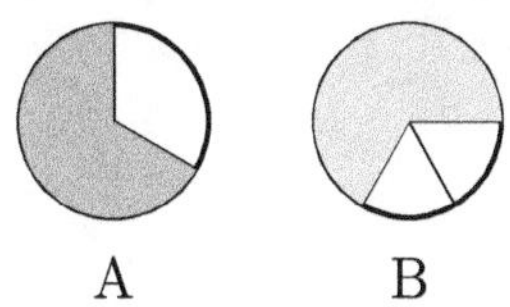

☐ A. Only Picture A shows $\frac{2}{3}$.
☐ B. Only Picture B shows $\frac{2}{3}$.
☐ C. Both show the same amount
☐ D. Neither

19) A book costs \$12.95 and a pen costs \$2.50. If you buy 3 books and 5 pens, what is the total cost?

☐ A. \$49.35 ☐ C. \$51.35
☐ B. \$53.35 ☐ D. \$55.35

20) On a time-temperature graph, the x-axis shows time in hours and the y-axis shows temperature in degrees Celsius. What does the point $(9, 15)$ mean?

☐ A. At hour 9, the temperature is 15 degrees Celsius.
☐ B. At hour 15, the temperature is 9 degrees Celsius.
☐ C. The temperature changes from 9 degrees to 15 degrees.
☐ D. The graph has 9 points and 15 labels.

21) A model shows 4 wholes, each cut into fifths. Which statements are true? *Select all that apply.*

4 wholes, each divided into fifths

☐ A. There are 20 fifth-size pieces. ☐ C. There are 16 fifth-size pieces.
☐ B. $4 \div \frac{1}{5} = 20$. ☐ D. $4 \div \frac{1}{5} = 16$.

22) A composite storage display is made from two non-overlapping rectangular prisms. Prism A is 8 feet long, 2 feet wide, and 3 feet tall. Prism B is 3 feet long, 5 feet wide, and 5 feet tall. What is the total volume?

☐ A. 48 cubic feet ☐ C. 123 cubic feet
☐ B. 75 cubic feet ☐ D. 139 cubic feet

23) A rectangular prism has length 9 cm, width 4 cm, and height 3 cm. What is its volume?

☐ A. 27 cm^3
☐ B. 36 cm^3
☐ C. 108 cm^3
☐ D. 216 cm^3

24) A metric conversion: 1.5 meters = ____ centimeters. (There are 100 cm in 1 m, so multiply by 100.) Which is correct?

☐ A. $1.5 \times 10 = 15$ cm
☐ B. $1.5 \div 100 = 0.015$ cm
☐ C. $1.5 \times 1000 = 1500$ cm
☐ D. $1.5 \times 100 = 150$ cm

25) Which shows the correct place-value shift for 42×10?

Hundreds	Tens	Ones	Result
4	2	0	420

☐ A. The 4 stays in hundreds, 2 moves to tens
☐ B. The 4 and 2 both move left one place, 0 fills ones
☐ C. The 4 stays in tens, 2 stays in ones, 0 fills hundreds
☐ D. All digits shift right by one place

26) Evaluate: $6 \times (7 + 3) - 20$

☐ A. 20
☐ B. 30
☐ C. 40
☐ D. 50

27) Which sum is correct?

Problem	Sum
A: $3.14 + 2.35$	5.59
B: $4.26 + 1.53$	5.79
C: $6.12 + 2.31$	8.53
D: $7.41 + 1.24$	8.75

☐ A. A
☐ B. B
☐ C. C
☐ D. D

28)

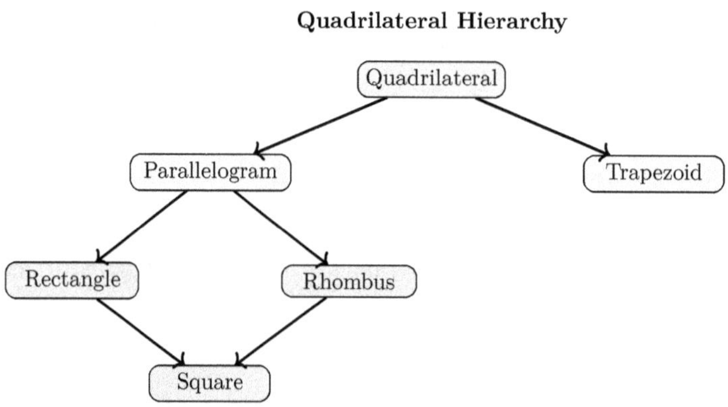

According to the hierarchy, which is true?

☐ A. Every rectangle is a square.
☐ B. Every parallelogram is a trapezoid.
☐ C. Every trapezoid is a parallelogram.
☐ D. Every square is a rectangle.

29) A swimmer has 5 miles of practice lanes to divide into $\frac{1}{4}$-mile repeats. How many repeats can she plan?

☐ A. $\frac{1}{4}$ repeat
☐ B. $\frac{3}{4}$ repeat
☐ C. $1\frac{3}{4}$ repeats
☐ D. 20 repeats

30) A track is $\frac{1}{4}$ kilometer long. If you run $\frac{3}{4}$ of the track, how far do you run?

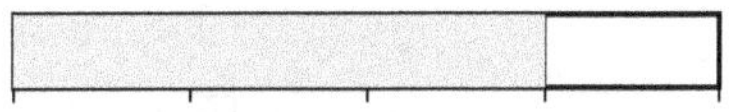

☐ A. $\frac{3}{16}$ km
☐ B. $\frac{1}{4}$ km
☐ C. $\frac{1}{2}$ km
☐ D. 1 km

31) A box of crayons has 36 crayons. If you use $\frac{2}{9}$ of them for a project, how many do you use?

☐ A. 4 crayons
☐ B. 8 crayons
☐ C. 18 crayons
☐ D. 28 crayons

32) A recipe calls for $\frac{1}{8}$ cup of sugar. The recipe is divided into 3 equal portions. How much sugar is needed for each portion?

☐ A. $\frac{1}{11}$ cup
☐ B. $\frac{3}{8}$ cup
☐ C. $\frac{1}{5}$ cup
☐ D. $\frac{1}{24}$ cup

33) Which statement is true?

☐ A. $\frac{1}{2} \times \frac{1}{3} = \frac{1}{5}$
☐ B. $\frac{2}{3} \times \frac{2}{3} = \frac{4}{6}$
☐ C. $\frac{3}{4} \times \frac{1}{4} = \frac{4}{16}$
☐ D. $\frac{1}{2} \times \frac{1}{2} = \frac{1}{4}$

34) A triangle has two sides of 10 m and one side of 6 m. What is it called based on sides, and what can you say about its angles?

☐ A. Scalene; angles unknown
☐ B. Isosceles; two angles equal
☐ C. Equilateral; all angles 60°
☐ D. Right; one angle 90°

35) A rectangular prism is built to be 3 units wide, 5 units long, and has a volume of 60 unit cubes. What is its height?

☐ A. 2 units
☐ B. 5 units
☐ C. 6 units
☐ D. 4 units

36) A storage room is 18 feet long, 12 feet wide, and 10 feet tall. If identical boxes each occupy 360 cubic feet and exactly fill the room with no gaps or overlaps, how many boxes fit in the storage room?

☐ A. 4 boxes
☐ B. 6 boxes
☐ C. 8 boxes
☐ D. 10 boxes

37) A point has a y-coordinate of 6. Its x-coordinate is half its y-coordinate. What is the ordered pair?

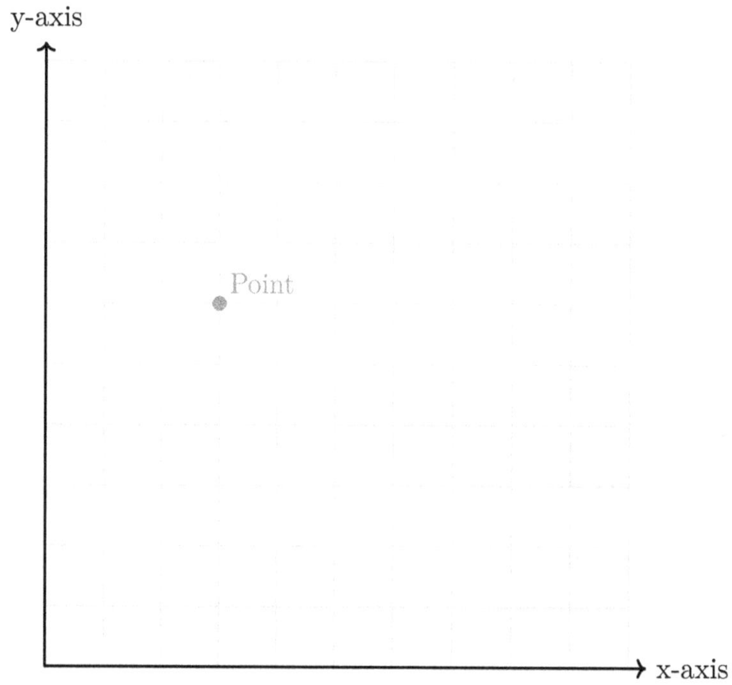

☐ A. $(6, 3)$
☐ B. $(3, 6)$
☐ C. $(12, 6)$
☐ D. $(2, 6)$

38) If 15.42−? = 8.67, what is the missing value?

☐ A. 7.15
☐ B. 6.85
☐ C. 6.75
☐ D. 7.25

39) The line plot shows 8 pencil lengths, in inches. What length appears most often?

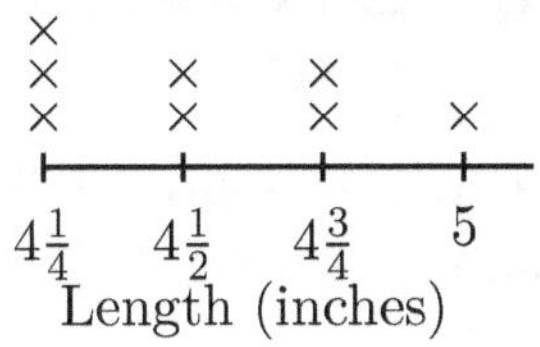

Record your answer in the space provided.

40) For a rectangular prism, the volume is 120 cubic units. The width is 5 units and the height is 4 units. What is the length?

☐ A. 2,400 units
☐ B. 20 units
☐ C. 111 units
☐ D. 6 units

End of Practice Test

Take a short breath, then check your work with care. Good corrections can teach almost as much as the test itself.

Precision Champion! ✓

You finished a full test. That takes focus and stamina.
Almost-right is still wrong. Train your eyes to see exactly.

Precision Beats Almost-Right ★

Mei loved math, but she sometimes lost points for tiny mistakes: a missing zero, a wrong decimal, a flipped negative.

She started a new habit: "finger-trace" the numbers she copied. With one finger on the page and her eyes following, she copied every digit exactly. The careless mistakes vanished.

On 5th grade tests, exact copying is a superpower. Numbers in the question must match numbers in your work. One small change, one wrong answer.

Math Mindset Tip: **Copy numbers carefully. Touch them with your eyes (or a fingertip).**

Precision turns hard work into the right answer.
— Math Mindset

Mei's Amazing Journey ★

Mei's secret wasn't speed. It was care. After she copied a number from the question to her work, she paused and read it back to make sure it matched. Imagine a problem with 1,204. If you write 1,240 instead, every step after that is wrong—even when the math is perfect.

Try Mei's check on the next test. Two seconds of care can save four big points.

Mei's Secret: **Copy every digit exactly. Your work depends on it.**

Try this on your next practice test. Small, smart habits become big score boosters.

★ Be precise. Be powerful. ★

Tiny care moments make giant score boosts.

Grade 5 Math

Grade 5 Mathematics

3

Questions: 40 **Duration:** No time limit

Calculator Policy: Calculators are not allowed

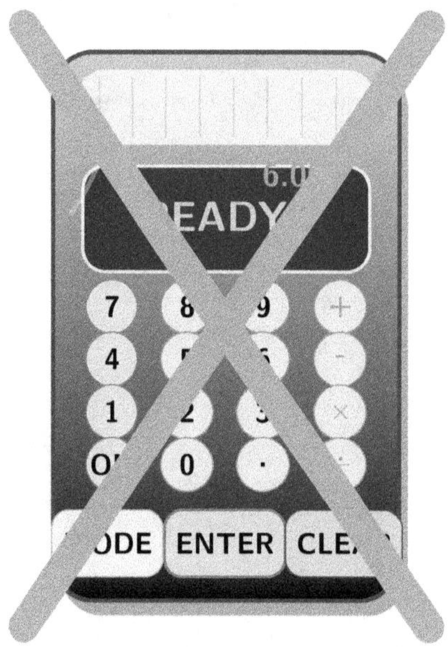

Grade 5 Mathematics Reference Materials

PERIMETER AND AREA

Perimeter of Rectangle	$P = 2l + 2w$ or $P = 2(l + w)$
Area of Rectangle	$A = l \times w$
Area of Triangle	$A = \frac{1}{2} \times b \times h$
Volume of Rectangular Prism	$V = l \times w \times h$

LENGTH

Customary	**Metric**
1 foot (ft) = 12 inches (in.)	1 meter (m) = 100 centimeters (cm)
1 yard (yd) = 3 feet (ft)	1 centimeter (cm) = 10 millimeters (mm)
1 yard (yd) = 36 inches (in.)	1 kilometer (km) = 1,000 meters (m)

CAPACITY

Customary	**Metric**
1 cup (c) = 8 fluid ounces (fl oz)	1 liter (L) = 1,000 milliliters (mL)
1 pint (pt) = 2 cups (c)	
1 quart (qt) = 2 pints (pt)	
1 gallon (gal) = 4 quarts (qt)	

WEIGHT AND MASS

Customary	**Metric**
1 pound (lb) = 16 ounces (oz)	1 kilogram (kg) = 1,000 grams (g)
	1 gram (g) = 1,000 milligrams (mg)

TIME

1 minute (min) = 60 seconds (sec)	1 week = 7 days
1 hour (hr) = 60 minutes (min)	1 year = 12 months
1 day = 24 hours (hr)	1 year = 52 weeks

1) In a Venn diagram with an outer circle and an inner circle, which labels make a correct relationship?

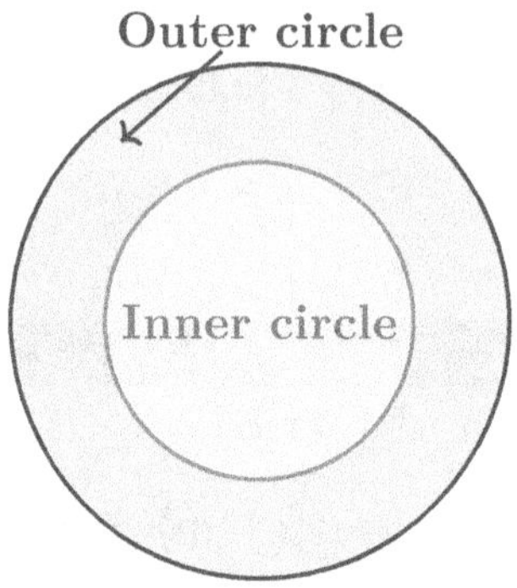

☐ A. Triangles inside quadrilaterals
☐ B. Circles inside polygons
☐ C. Pentagons inside quadrilaterals
☐ D. Rectangles inside parallelograms

2) Which decimal represents "two and thirty-seven hundredths"?

☐ A. 0.237
☐ B. 2.037
☐ C. 23.7
☐ D. 2.37

3) Estimate $5\frac{1}{6} + 2\frac{7}{8}$ by rounding each mixed number to the nearest whole number.

Record your answer in the space provided.

4) Which expression does NOT equal 0.73?

☐ A. $73 \div 100$
☐ B. $7.3 \div 10$
☐ C. $730 \div 1000$
☐ D. $73 \div 10$

5) A strip shows one eighth split into 3 equal parts. Which equation matches the model?

☐ A. $3 \div \frac{1}{8} =?$

☐ B. $\frac{1}{8} \times 3 =?$

☐ C. $\frac{1}{8} \div 3 =?$

☐ D. $3 + \frac{1}{8} =?$

6) A bottle holds 2 liters of juice. Each cup holds one fifth liter. Which division equation matches the situation?

☐ A. $\frac{1}{5} \div 2 = n$

☐ B. $2 \div \frac{1}{5} = n$

☐ C. $2 \times \frac{1}{5} = n$

☐ D. $2 + \frac{1}{5} = n$

7) The line plot shows the number of points scored in video games:

Video Game Scores

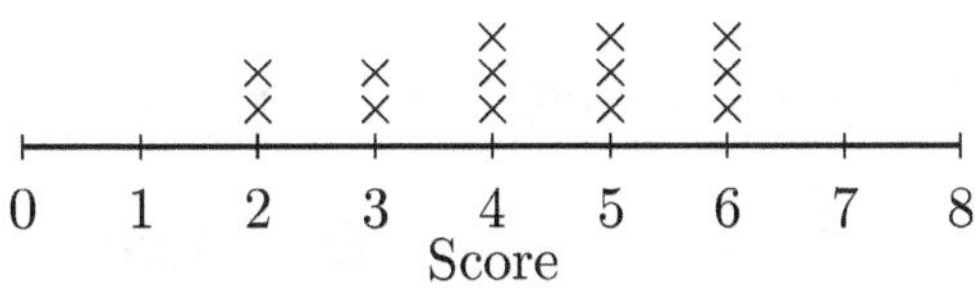

What is the difference between the highest and lowest scores?

☐ A. 2

☐ B. 3

☐ C. 4

☐ D. 5

8) The line plot shows lengths of ribbon pieces, in inches:

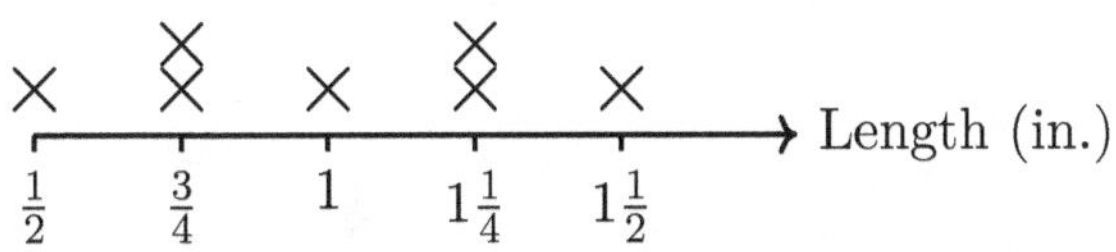

What is the total length of the pieces longer than 1 inch?

☐ A. $2\frac{3}{4}$ inches

☐ B. $6\frac{1}{2}$ inches

☐ C. 5 inches

☐ D. 4 inches

9) What is $5 \times \frac{2}{7}$?

☐ A. $\frac{2}{35}$
☐ B. $\frac{10}{7}$
☐ C. $\frac{7}{10}$
☐ D. $\frac{2}{12}$

10) Which statement is true?

☐ A. $\frac{2}{3} + \frac{3}{4} = \frac{5}{7}$
☐ B. $\frac{2}{3} + \frac{3}{4} = 1\frac{5}{12}$
☐ C. $\frac{2}{3} + \frac{3}{4} = 1$ whole
☐ D. $\frac{2}{3} + \frac{3}{4} = \frac{6}{12}$

11) Without calculating, how does $(18 \times 5) + 3$ compare with 18×5?

☐ A. 3 less
☐ B. $\frac{1}{3}$ as large
☐ C. 3 times as large
☐ D. 3 more

12) How many feet are in 54 inches? (Express as a mixed number if needed.)

☐ A. $5\frac{1}{2}$ feet
☐ B. $4\frac{3}{4}$ feet
☐ C. 5 feet
☐ D. $4\frac{1}{2}$ feet

13) Subtract: $\frac{8}{10} - \frac{1}{5}$

☐ A. $\frac{7}{10}$
☐ B. $\frac{6}{10} = \frac{3}{5}$
☐ C. $\frac{6}{15}$
☐ D. $\frac{1}{5}$

14) The area of a square is found by multiplying side length by itself. If each side is $1\frac{1}{2}$ inches, what is the area?

	1	$\frac{1}{2}$
1	1	$\frac{1}{2}$
$\frac{1}{2}$	$\frac{1}{2}$	$\frac{1}{4}$

Area: $1\frac{1}{2}$ in $\times$ $1\frac{1}{2}$ in gives square inches

☐ A. $3\frac{1}{4}$ square inches
☐ B. 3 square inches
☐ C. $2\frac{1}{4}$ square inches
☐ D. $1\frac{1}{2}$ square inches

15) Estimate $2,345 \div 59$ using compatible numbers:

☐ A. $2,400 \div 60 = 40$
☐ B. $2,100 \div 70 = 30$
☐ C. $2,000 \div 50 = 40$
☐ D. $2,500 \div 75 = 33$

16) Which of these equals 6,000?

☐ A. 6×100
☐ B. 60×10
☐ C. 300×20
☐ D. 600×100

17) What is $1.2 \div 0.3$?

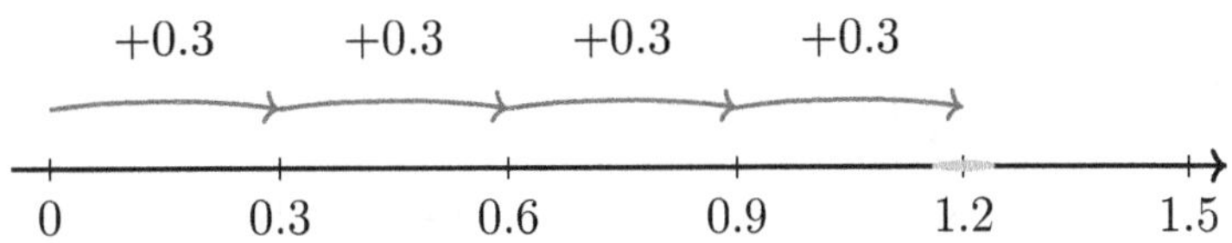

☐ A. 3
☐ B. 6
☐ C. 5
☐ D. 4

18) From the pattern "add 3, start at 2", list ordered pairs (index, value) for indices 1–4:

☐ A. $(1,2),(2,5),(3,8),(4,11)$
☐ B. $(1,5),(2,8),(3,11),(4,14)$
☐ C. $(2,1),(5,2),(8,3),(11,4)$
☐ D. $(1,3),(2,6),(3,9),(4,12)$

19) A scientist measures three liquid samples: Sample A is 0.8 L, Sample B is 850 mL, and Sample C is 0.75 L. Which sample is the smallest?

☐ A. Sample A (0.8 L)
☐ B. Sample B (850 mL)
☐ C. Sample C (0.75 L)
☐ D. Samples A and C are equal

20) For the point $(4, 3)$, which statements are true? *Select all that apply.*

- ☐ A. Move 4 right from the origin.
- ☐ B. Move 3 up from the origin.
- ☐ C. Move 3 right from the origin.
- ☐ D. Move 4 up from the origin.

21) Evaluate the expression: $100 - (8 \times 6) - 2 \times 5$

Record your answer in the space provided.

22) A group of 6 friends shares the total cost of a \$42 gift and a \$3 card. Which expression gives each friend's share?

- ☐ A. $(42 + 3) \div 6$
- ☐ B. $42 \div 6 + 3$
- ☐ C. $(42 - 3) \div 6$
- ☐ D. $42 + 3 \div 6$

23) A plank of wood is $13\frac{3}{4}$ feet long. A carpenter cuts off a piece $6\frac{5}{8}$ feet long. (First, express with common denominator.) How much wood remains?

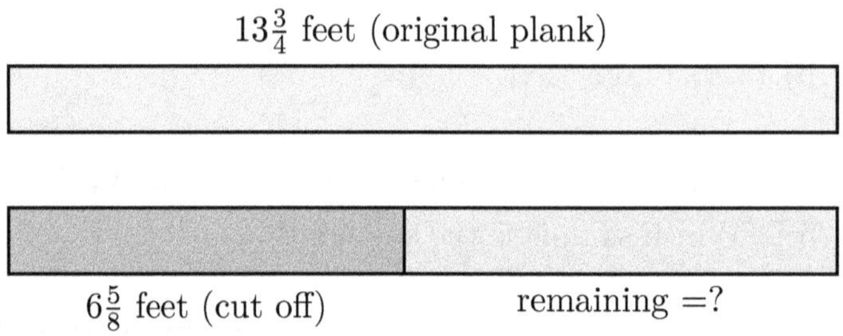

- ☐ A. $7\frac{1}{8}$ ft
- ☐ B. $7\frac{1}{4}$ ft
- ☐ C. $6\frac{3}{8}$ ft
- ☐ D. $6\frac{5}{8}$ ft

24) Find: $7 \div \frac{1}{6}$.

Record your answer in the space provided.

25) A science kit box measures 6 meters long, 7 meters wide, and 7 meters tall. What is its volume?

- ☐ A. 42 cubic meters
- ☐ B. 49 cubic meters
- ☐ C. 20 cubic meters
- ☐ D. 294 cubic meters

26) A cubic meter is made of how many cubic centimeters?

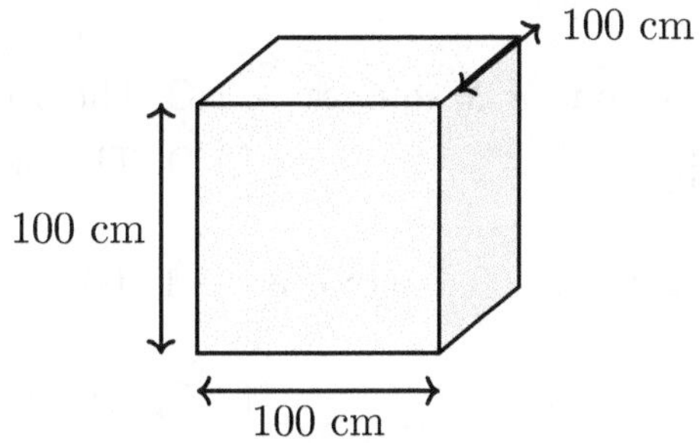

1 m = 100 cm

- ☐ A. 100
- ☐ B. 1,000
- ☐ C. 100,000
- ☐ D. 1,000,000

27) Compare using <, >, or =: 0.342 ____ 0.386.

Record your answer in the space provided.

28) A kitchen scale shows weights in grams. Three ingredients are measured: Salt: 25 grams, Sugar: 50 grams, Flour: 225 grams.
How many kilograms is the total weight?

☐ A. 0.03 kilograms
☐ B. 30 kilograms
☐ C. 3 kilograms
☐ D. 0.3 kilograms

29) Below is an area model for $\frac{2}{5} \times \frac{3}{4}$. Which statement is true?

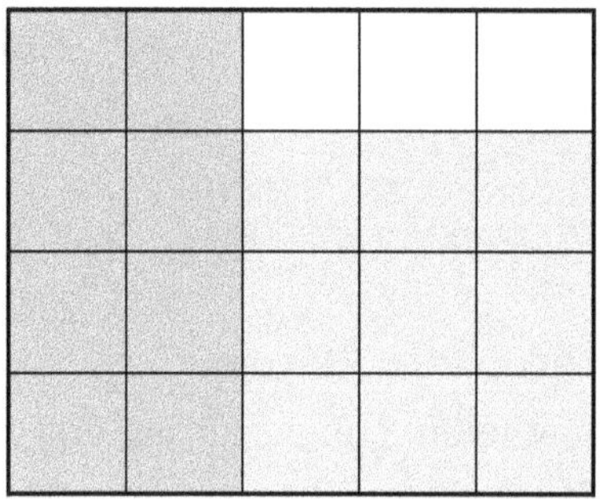

☐ A. The overlap covers 6 out of 20 squares.
☐ B. The product is $\frac{5}{9}$.
☐ C. The overlap covers 6 out of 12 squares.
☐ D. The product is $\frac{2}{4}$.

30) Pattern: $8.1 \div 10 = 0.81$; $8.1 \div 100 = 0.081$; $8.1 \div 1{,}000 = ?$

☐ A. 81
☐ B. 0.081
☐ C. 8.1
☐ D. 0.0081

31) Which statement is true?

☐ A. $10^3 > 10^4$
☐ B. $10^2 = 1000$
☐ C. $10^5 < 10^6$
☐ D. $10^1 = 100$

32) Tom had $4\frac{1}{2}$ feet of rope and used $1\frac{3}{4}$ feet. How much rope is left?

Record your answer in the space provided.

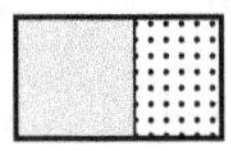

$1\frac{3}{4}$

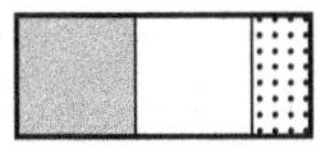

$2\frac{1}{2}$

33)

Add: $1\frac{3}{4} + 2\frac{1}{2}$

- ☐ A. $3\frac{1}{4}$
- ☐ B. $4\frac{1}{4}$
- ☐ C. $4\frac{3}{4}$
- ☐ D. $3\frac{1}{2}$

34) Which student found the correct answer to $5,200 \div 100$?

Student	Answer
Marcus	520
Jenna	52
Kevin	5.2
Aisha	5,200

- ☐ A. Marcus
- ☐ B. Jenna
- ☐ C. Kevin
- ☐ D. Aisha

35) Which number is closest to 0.5 on a number line?

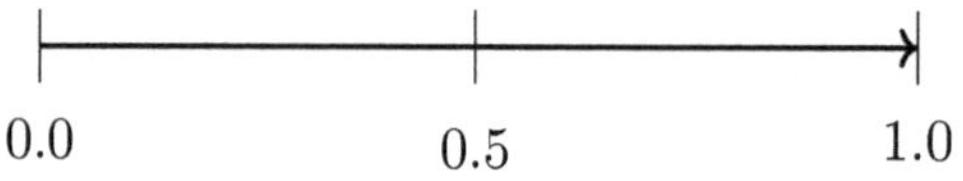

☐ A. 0.45
☐ B. 0.489
☐ C. 0.501
☐ D. 0.55

36)

Student	Method for 21×13	Answer
Riley	$(20 + 1) \times 13$	273
Jamal	$21 \times (10 + 3)$	273
Piper	Area model with 4 parts	260

Which student or students found the correct answer to 21×13?

☐ A. Only Riley
☐ B. Only Jamal
☐ C. Riley and Jamal
☐ D. Only Piper

37) Three points are listed: (1, 4), (2, 8), and (3, 12). What is the relationship?

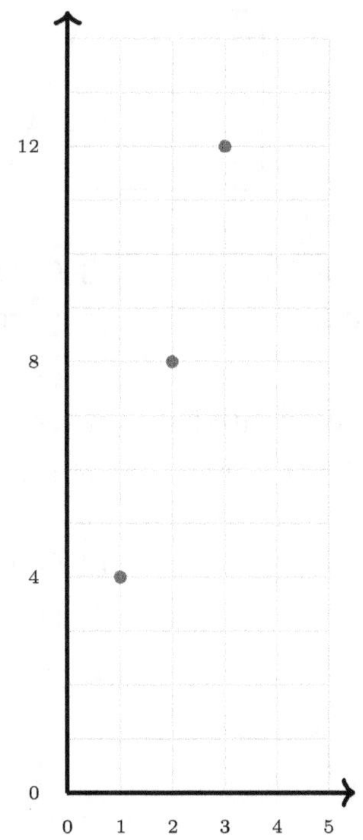

- ☐ A. The second coordinate is triple the first, then 1 more
- ☐ B. The second coordinate is 4 more than the first
- ☐ C. The second coordinate is double the first, then 2 more
- ☐ D. The second coordinate is 4 times the first

38) Pattern: $8, 16, 24, 32, \ldots$ vs. Pattern: $8, 16, 32, 64, \ldots$ Which statement is true?

- ☐ A. Both patterns have the same 5th term
- ☐ B. The first pattern adds 8 each time; the second multiplies by 2
- ☐ C. Both are doubling patterns
- ☐ D. The second pattern adds 8 each time

39) Look at the figure. Which statement about the angles is correct?

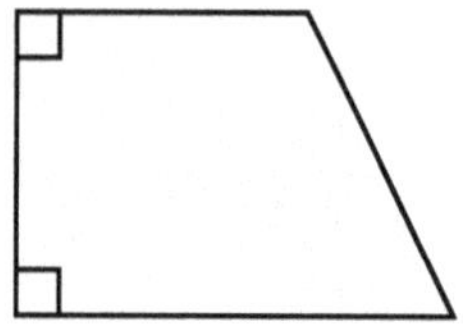

☐ A. All four angles are right angles.
☐ B. No angles are right angles.
☐ C. One angle is right angle.
☐ D. Two angles are right angles.

40) **Error Analysis:** A student calculated that a rectangular prism with volume 160 cm^3, length 8 cm, and width 5 cm has height 6 cm. Is the student correct?

☐ A. No; height is 4 cm
☐ B. Yes, correct
☐ C. No; height is 5 cm
☐ D. No; height is 7 cm

End of Practice Test

Take a short breath, then check your work with care. Good corrections can teach almost as much as the test itself.

Plan-First Star! ✓

You finished a full test. That takes focus and stamina.
A short plan saves a long detour.

Plan Before You Solve ★

Ada Lovelace is often called the first computer programmer. Her superpower? Planning. She wrote down the steps before she ever ran the program.

You can do the same on a math test. Before you compute, write a tiny plan: 1) Find the question. 2) Pick the operation. 3) Check the units.

It feels slow at first, but the plan is the speed. You skip dead ends and head straight for the answer.

Math Mindset Tip: **A 5-second plan saves a 30-second detour.**

First plan, then solve. The plan is the shortcut.
— *Math Mindset*

Lovelace's Amazing Journey ★

Ada planned because she knew that one missed step could ruin a whole program. The same is true in math.

On a multi-step word problem, missing a step (like a unit conversion or a final addition) costs the whole answer. Planning fixes that.

Try this: before any multi-step problem, write "Step 1, Step 2, Step 3" in the margin. Then solve.

Lovelace's Secret: **Steps in the margin are guardrails for your brain.**

Try this on your next practice test. Small, smart habits become big score boosters.

★ **Plan it. Solve it. Check it.** ★

Small planning, giant payoff.

Grade 5 Math

Grade 5 Mathematics

4

Questions: 40 Duration: No time limit

Calculator Policy: Calculators are not allowed

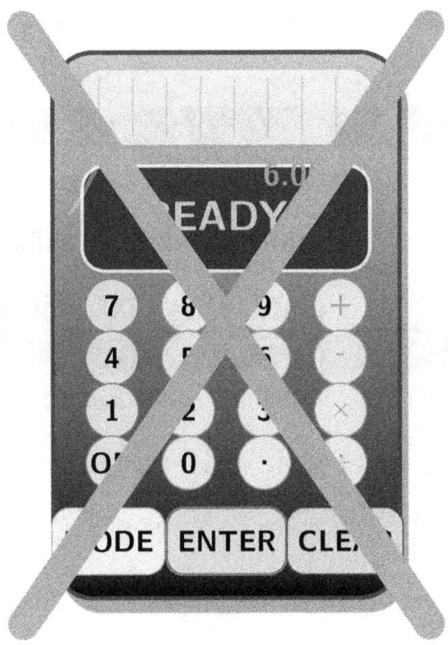

Grade 5 Mathematics Reference Materials

PERIMETER AND AREA

Perimeter of Rectangle	$P = 2l + 2w$ or $P = 2(l + w)$
Area of Rectangle	$A = l \times w$
Area of Triangle	$A = \frac{1}{2} \times b \times h$
Volume of Rectangular Prism	$V = l \times w \times h$

LENGTH

Customary	**Metric**
1 foot (ft) = 12 inches (in.)	1 meter (m) = 100 centimeters (cm)
1 yard (yd) = 3 feet (ft)	1 centimeter (cm) = 10 millimeters (mm)
1 yard (yd) = 36 inches (in.)	1 kilometer (km) = 1,000 meters (m)

CAPACITY

Customary	**Metric**
1 cup (c) = 8 fluid ounces (fl oz)	1 liter (L) = 1,000 milliliters (mL)
1 pint (pt) = 2 cups (c)	
1 quart (qt) = 2 pints (pt)	
1 gallon (gal) = 4 quarts (qt)	

WEIGHT AND MASS

Customary	**Metric**
1 pound (lb) = 16 ounces (oz)	1 kilogram (kg) = 1,000 grams (g)
	1 gram (g) = 1,000 milligrams (mg)

TIME

1 minute (min) = 60 seconds (sec)	1 week = 7 days
1 hour (hr) = 60 minutes (min)	1 year = 12 months
1 day = 24 hours (hr)	1 year = 52 weeks

1) A concrete block is 12 in. × 8 in. × 4 in.. Which unit should be used to describe the amount of space the block occupies?

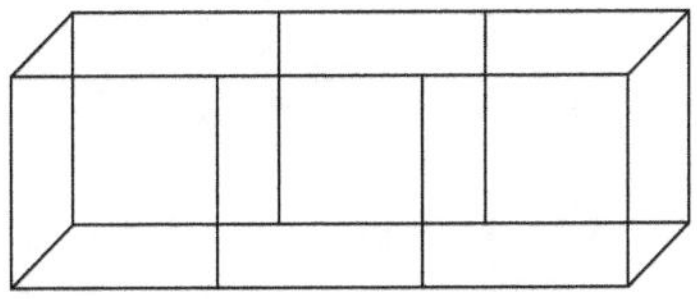

Block: 12 × 8 × 4 in.

☐ A. inches
☐ B. square inches
☐ C. cubic inches
☐ D. pounds

2) Without calculating, which is smallest?

☐ A. 8 × 9
☐ B. 8 × 7
☐ C. 7 × 9
☐ D. 7 × 7

3) A solid is made from two non-overlapping rectangular prisms. One prism is 6 m by 4 m by 4 m. The other is 6 m by 4 m by 3 m. What is the total volume?

☐ A. 168 cubic meters
☐ B. 144 cubic meters
☐ C. 112 cubic meters
☐ D. 280 cubic meters

4) A triangle has one angle that measures 120 degrees. What type of triangle is this based on its angles?

☐ A. Acute triangle
☐ B. Right triangle
☐ C. Scalene triangle
☐ D. Obtuse triangle

5) The expression tree shows how to evaluate the grouped expression $((8+2)\times(7-3))$. What is the final value?

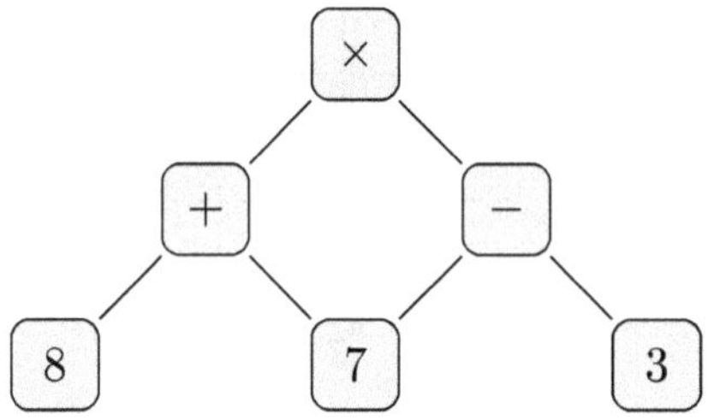

- ☐ A. 30
- ☐ B. 60
- ☐ C. 50
- ☐ D. 40

6) Find: $1\dfrac{1}{2} \times 2\dfrac{1}{3}$.

Record your answer in the space provided.

7) Write $4 + \frac{7}{10} + \frac{1}{100}$ as a decimal.

- ☐ A. 4.17
- ☐ B. 47.1
- ☐ C. 0.471
- ☐ D. 4.71

8) Compare $\frac{3}{2} \times 18$ to 18. Which is true?

- ☐ A. $\frac{3}{2} \times 18 < 18$
- ☐ B. $\frac{3}{2} \times 18 = 18$
- ☐ C. $\frac{3}{2} \times 18 > 18$
- ☐ D. Cannot be determined

9) A library fundraiser collected three donations: \$284.75, \$156.50, and \$320.25. The library spends \$450.00 on new books. How much money is left?

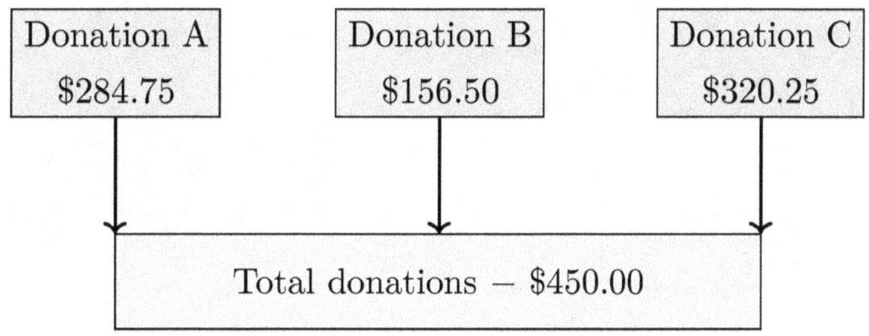

☐ A. \$301.50
☐ B. \$761.50
☐ C. \$321.50
☐ D. \$311.50

10) On a time-distance graph, the x-axis shows time in hours and the y-axis shows distance in miles. A point is plotted on the graph. What does the plotted point represent?

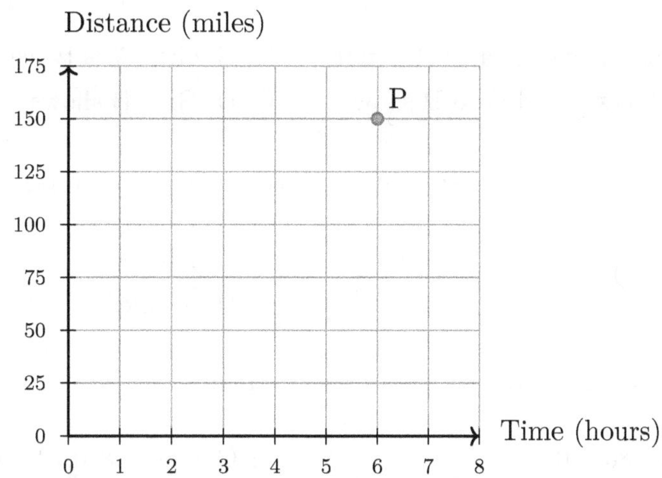

☐ A. 6 hours, 150 miles
☐ B. 150 hours, 6 miles
☐ C. 150 hours, 150 miles
☐ D. 6 hours, 6 miles

11) Compare the two 10 by 10 grids. Grid A has 20 squares shaded; Grid B has 40 squares shaded. Which statement is true?

Grid A: $\frac{20}{100}$

Grid B: $\frac{40}{100}$

- ☐ A. Both grids show equivalent fractions
- ☐ B. Grid A shows $\frac{1}{5}$ and Grid B shows $\frac{2}{5}$
- ☐ C. Grid A is twice as much as Grid B
- ☐ D. Grid B shows $\frac{1}{5}$ and Grid A shows $\frac{2}{5}$

12) A hiker climbs $\frac{3}{4}$ mile uphill, rests, then climbs $\frac{2}{8}$ mile more. Total distance?

- ☐ A. $\frac{1}{2}$ mile
- ☐ B. $\frac{5}{8}$ mile
- ☐ C. 1 mile
- ☐ D. $\frac{7}{8}$ mile

13) Which set of decimals is ordered from least to greatest?

- ☐ A. $0.8, 0.72, 0.86, 1.0$
- ☐ B. $0.72, 0.8, 0.86, 1.0$
- ☐ C. $0.86, 0.8, 0.72, 1.0$
- ☐ D. $1.0, 0.86, 0.8, 0.72$

14) Find: $480 \div 10$.

Record your answer in the space provided.

15) The line plot shows flour amounts, in cups, used in recipes:

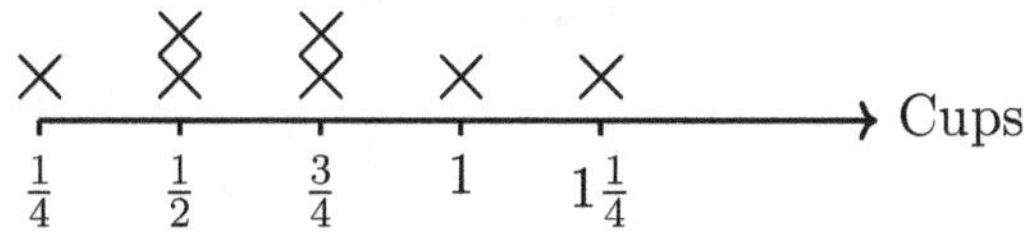

What is the total amount of flour shown?

☐ A. $3\frac{1}{2}$ cups
☐ B. $4\frac{3}{4}$ cups
☐ C. 5 cups
☐ D. $5\frac{1}{2}$ cups

16) Population fact: A town has 1.25 thousand people. How many people is that in total?

☐ A. 125
☐ B. 125000
☐ C. 12500
☐ D. 1250

17) A box with volume 56 unit cubes has a length of 7 units and a width of 4 units. What is its height?

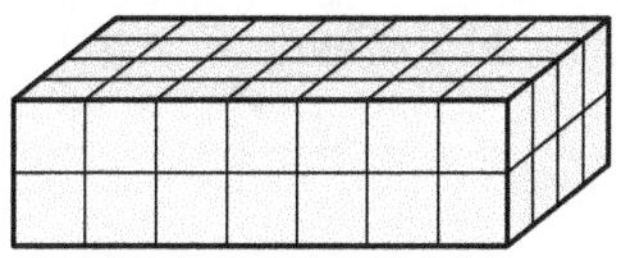

☐ A. 1 unit
☐ B. 3 units
☐ C. 8 units
☐ D. 2 units

18) The line plot shows plant growth measurements, in inches:

Plant Growth

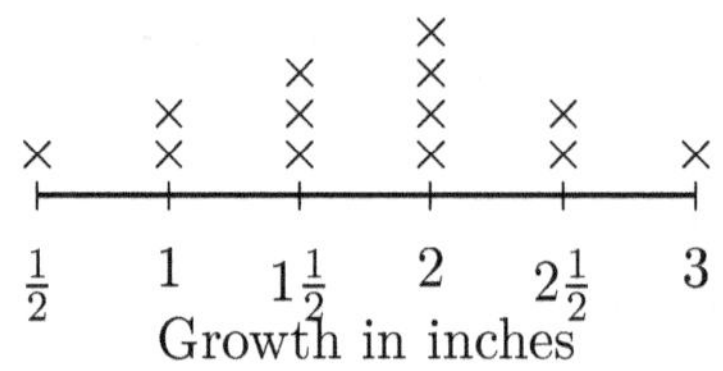

How many measurements were 2 inches or longer?

- ☐ A. 4
- ☐ B. 5
- ☐ C. 6
- ☐ D. 7

19) Pattern M: $0, 5, 10, 15, \ldots$ Pattern N: $0, 10, 20, 30, \ldots$ Which statements describe their relationship? *Select all that apply.*

- ☐ A. Each term of N is twice the matching term of M.
- ☐ B. Pattern N is twice Pattern M for each matching pair.
- ☐ C. N grows slower than M.
- ☐ D. M and N have the same 4th term.

20) A student says $1.75 + 2.38 = 3.113$. What is the main error?

- ☐ A. The student forgot to regroup 113 hundredths.
- ☐ B. The student should have rounded before adding.
- ☐ C. The student got 4.13, which is correct.
- ☐ D. The student should have subtracted instead of added.

no right angles

opposite sides are parallel

21) The opposite sides are parallel, and no angles are right angles. Which statement is TRUE?

- ☐ A. This must be a rectangle because it has four sides.
- ☐ B. This cannot be a quadrilateral.
- ☐ C. This is a trapezoid because sides are not equal.
- ☐ D. This is a parallelogram but NOT a rectangle.

22) A swimming pool is 25 m long, 10 m wide, 2 m deep. Find its volume.

Record your answer in the space provided.

23) A jug has 10 liters of water. Each bottle holds one fifth liter. Which division equation matches the situation?

- ☐ A. $\frac{1}{5} \div 10 = n$
- ☐ B. $10 \times \frac{1}{5} = n$
- ☐ C. $10 + \frac{1}{5} = n$
- ☐ D. $10 \div \frac{1}{5} = n$

24) Which expression has a sum close to 2?

- ☐ A. $\frac{1}{10} + \frac{3}{11}$
- ☐ B. $1\frac{1}{12} + \frac{7}{8}$
- ☐ C. $\frac{2}{9} + \frac{1}{7}$
- ☐ D. $\frac{4}{5} + \frac{1}{12}$

25) What is $6 \div \frac{1}{2}$?

☐ A. 12
☐ B. 3
☐ C. 6
☐ D. 18

26)

Starting Number	Operation	Result
25.4	$\div 10$	?

What is the result?

☐ A. 254
☐ B. 0.254
☐ C. 2540
☐ D. 2.54

27) Four points are plotted: $(2, 2)$, $(8, 2)$, $(8, 8)$, and $(2, 8)$. What is the most specific name for the shape they form?

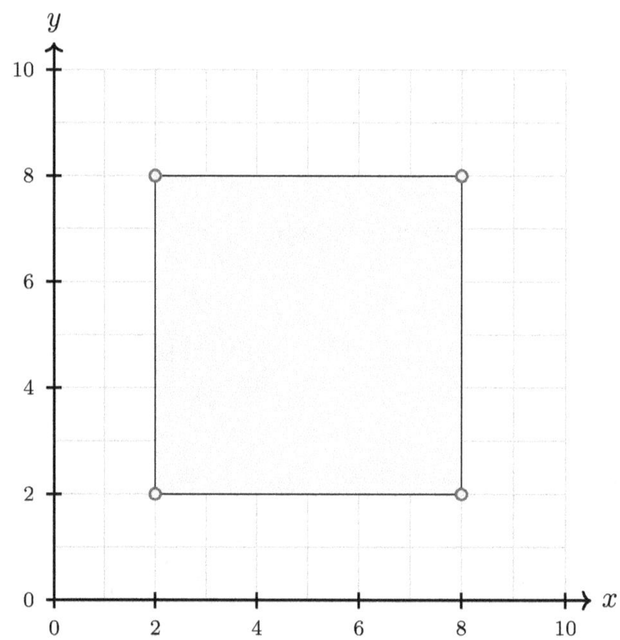

☐ A. Square
☐ B. Rectangle
☐ C. Trapezoid
☐ D. Parallelogram

28) A concrete block measures 10 inches long, 8 inches wide, and 4 inches high. What is the volume?

☐ A. 280 in^3
☐ B. 320 in^3
☐ C. 360 in^3
☐ D. 400 in^3

29) Find the product: $80 \times 9{,}000$.

Record your answer in the space provided.

30) A farmer plants corn on $\frac{7}{12}$ of a field. She waters $\frac{1}{4}$ of the corn section. What fraction of the whole field is watered? Give the answer in simplest form.

☐ A. $\frac{7}{48}$ of the field
☐ B. $\frac{8}{16}$ of the field
☐ C. $\frac{2}{3}$ of the field
☐ D. $\frac{5}{6}$ of the field

31) A track is $\frac{1}{4}$ kilometer long. A student runs the track 8 times. How far does the student run?

☐ A. 2 km
☐ B. $\frac{1}{32}$ km
☐ C. $\frac{8}{1}$ km
☐ D. 1 km

32) Which of these correctly represents dividing $\frac{1}{3}$ into 3 equal parts?

☐ A. $\frac{1}{3} + 3$
☐ B. $\frac{1}{3} \div 3$
☐ C. $3 - \frac{1}{3}$
☐ D. $\frac{1}{3} \times 3$

33) A concert booth has 30 yards of wristband ribbon. Each wristband uses $\frac{1}{5}$ yard. How many wristbands can be made?

Sample yards divided into fifth-yard lengths

Only 5 of the 30 yards are shown

☐ A. 100 wristbands

☐ B. 120 wristbands

☐ C. 150 wristbands

☐ D. 180 wristbands

34) Area model showing overlap. Count total cells and shaded cells for $\frac{5}{6} \times \frac{3}{4}$.

$\frac{5}{6} \times \frac{3}{4}$

☐ A. Total: 24 cells; Shaded: 15

☐ B. Total: 20 cells; Shaded: 10

☐ C. Total: 24 cells; Shaded: 20

☐ D. Total: 30 cells; Shaded: 15

35) How many $\frac{1}{4}$-cup scoops are in 6 cups?

Record your answer in the space provided.

36) Evaluate: $100 \div (20 - 15) + 4$

☐ A. 24
☐ B. 9
☐ C. 14
☐ D. 20

37) A sporting goods company ships items in cartons of 100. To ship 4200 items, how many cartons are needed?

☐ A. 42
☐ B. 100
☐ C. 4200
☐ D. 420000

38) At a grocery store, you have \$32.58. You buy milk for \$4.75 and bread for \$2.89. How much money is left?

☐ A. \$24.84
☐ B. \$24.94
☐ C. \$25.04
☐ D. \$24.64

39)

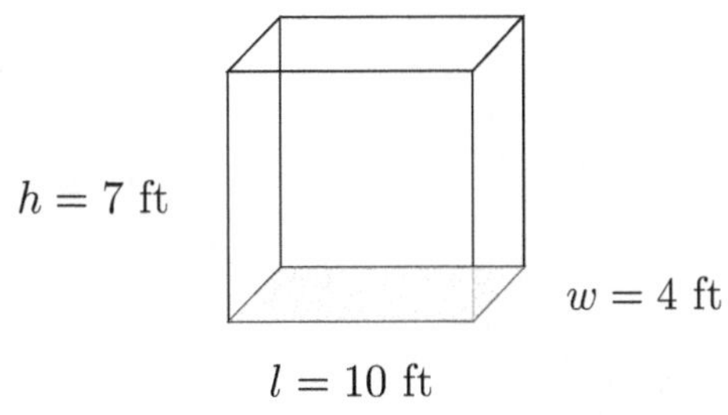

Calculate the volume.

☐ A. 280 ft^3
☐ B. 21 ft^3
☐ C. 40 ft^3
☐ D. 70 ft^3

40) Which point is farther up from the x-axis: $(6,4)$ or $(3,8)$?

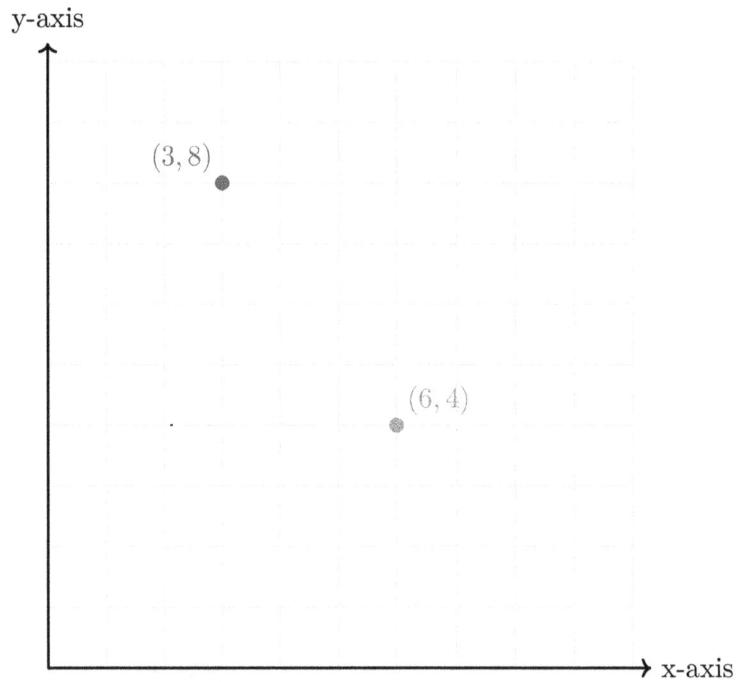

☐ A. $(6,4)$ is farther up

☐ B. $(3,8)$ is farther up

☐ C. They are the same height

☐ D. Cannot be determined

End of Practice Test

Take a short breath, then check your work with care. Good corrections can teach almost as much as the test itself.

Neat Notation Wins! ✓

You finished a full test. That takes focus and stamina.
Clear writing helps your brain see the answer.

Clear Notation Saves Points ★

Gottfried Leibniz invented many of the math symbols you use today, like the ÷ sign and clear ways to write fractions. He believed clear notation makes thinking easier.

Have you ever written a number sloppily, then misread your own "4" as a "9"? That's a notation mistake, not a math mistake. Leibniz would say, "Write so your future-self can read it."

On 5th grade tests, clear digits, neatly stacked numbers, and labeled units (cm, dollars) prevent silly mistakes that cost real points.

Math Mindset Tip: **Write neatly, line up your columns, and label your units. Your eyes will thank you.**

Clear writing is half the answer.
— Math Mindset

Leibniz's Amazing Journey ★

Leibniz cared about symbols because symbols carry meaning. A messy "7" that looks like a "1" can ruin a perfect plan.

Try this: when you copy a number, slow down and check that every digit is clear. When you set up multi-digit multiplication, line up your places. When you record an answer, include the unit.

These tiny habits will earn you more points than any new trick.

Leibniz's Secret: **Notation is part of math—don't skip it.**

Try this on your next practice test. Small, smart habits become big score boosters.

★ Write it clearly. Solve it clearly. ★

Neat notation is silent extra credit.

Grade 5 Math

Grade 5 Mathematics

5

Questions: 40 **Duration:** No time limit

Calculator Policy: Calculators are not allowed

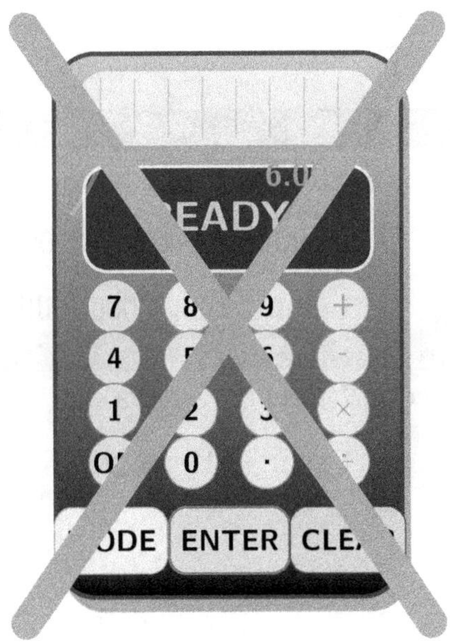

Grade 5 Mathematics Reference Materials

PERIMETER AND AREA

Perimeter of Rectangle	$P = 2l + 2w$ or $P = 2(l + w)$
Area of Rectangle	$A = l \times w$
Area of Triangle	$A = \frac{1}{2} \times b \times h$
Volume of Rectangular Prism	$V = l \times w \times h$

LENGTH

Customary	**Metric**
1 foot (ft) = 12 inches (in.)	1 meter (m) = 100 centimeters (cm)
1 yard (yd) = 3 feet (ft)	1 centimeter (cm) = 10 millimeters (mm)
1 yard (yd) = 36 inches (in.)	1 kilometer (km) = 1,000 meters (m)

CAPACITY

Customary	**Metric**
1 cup (c) = 8 fluid ounces (fl oz)	1 liter (L) = 1,000 milliliters (mL)
1 pint (pt) = 2 cups (c)	
1 quart (qt) = 2 pints (pt)	
1 gallon (gal) = 4 quarts (qt)	

WEIGHT AND MASS

Customary	**Metric**
1 pound (lb) = 16 ounces (oz)	1 kilogram (kg) = 1,000 grams (g)
	1 gram (g) = 1,000 milligrams (mg)

TIME

1 minute (min) = 60 seconds (sec)	1 week = 7 days
1 hour (hr) = 60 minutes (min)	1 year = 12 months
1 day = 24 hours (hr)	1 year = 52 weeks

1) Which pair shows products that are equal?

$6 \times \frac{3}{3}$	6×1

Are these equal?

- ☐ A. Cannot be determined
- ☐ B. No, first is bigger
- ☐ C. No, second is bigger
- ☐ D. Yes, both equal 6

2) A road sign shows two distances. One road is $\frac{7}{12}$ mile to the village and another is $\frac{1}{4}$ mile to the store. What is the combined distance?

- ☐ A. $\frac{8}{16}$ mile
- ☐ B. $\frac{9}{12}$ mile
- ☐ C. $\frac{10}{16}$ mile
- ☐ D. $\frac{5}{6}$ mile

3) Two patterns are shown using an input-output table. Input: 2, 4, 6, 8. Output: 10, 20, 30, 40. What is the rule?

- ☐ A. Output = Input +8
- ☐ B. Output = Input ×5
- ☐ C. Output = Input ×4
- ☐ D. Output = Input +5

4) Compare the fractions $\frac{2}{5}$ and $\frac{1}{3}$ by finding a common denominator. Which statement is true?

- ☐ A. $\frac{2}{5} < \frac{1}{3}$
- ☐ B. $\frac{2}{5} > \frac{1}{3}$
- ☐ C. $\frac{2}{5} = \frac{1}{3}$
- ☐ D. Cannot compare

5) A pattern starts at 50 and subtracts 3 each step. What is the 10th term?

- ☐ A. 23
- ☐ B. 20
- ☐ C. 17
- ☐ D. 30

6) A rectangular prism has volume 252 cm^3. Its length is 18 cm and width is 7 cm. What is its height?

- ☐ A. 3 cm
- ☐ B. 2 cm
- ☐ C. 4 cm
- ☐ D. 5 cm

7) The diagram compares two expressions. Which description fits Expression B relative to Expression A?

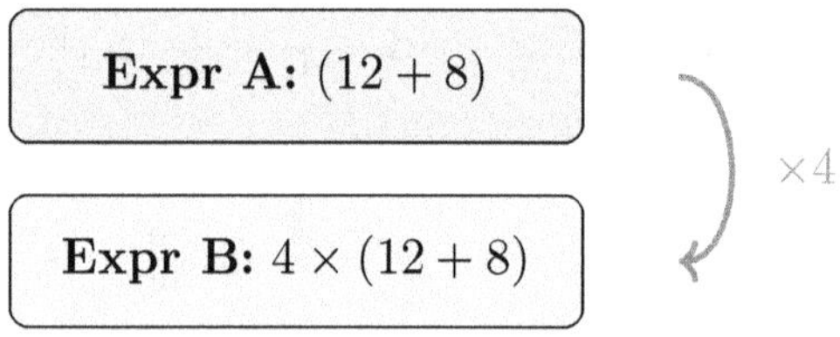

- ☐ A. 4 more than A
- ☐ B. 4 times as much as A
- ☐ C. $\frac{1}{4}$ of A
- ☐ D. 4 less than A

8) A stage block measures 9 centimeters long, 7 centimeters wide, and 7 centimeters tall. What is its volume?

- ☐ A. 441 cubic centimeters
- ☐ B. 63 cubic centimeters
- ☐ C. 49 cubic centimeters
- ☐ D. 23 cubic centimeters

9) Write the number that is 10 times 0.045.

Record your answer in the space provided.

10) A park path is 2 kilometers long. If a jogger has run 1,200 meters so far, how many more meters must they run to complete the path?

☐ A. 800 m
☐ B. 1,000 m
☐ C. 1,200 m
☐ D. 2,800 m

11) Two cyclists ride along straight paths. One rides 15.5 km, then another 8.25 km. The other rides 9.75 km, then 12 km. Who traveled farther in total, and by how much?

☐ A. First cyclist by 1.5 km
☐ B. Second cyclist by 2 km
☐ C. First cyclist by 2 km
☐ D. They traveled equal distances

12) A graph displays the first three points in a pattern: (1, 5), (2, 7), and (3, 9). Which point should be plotted next?

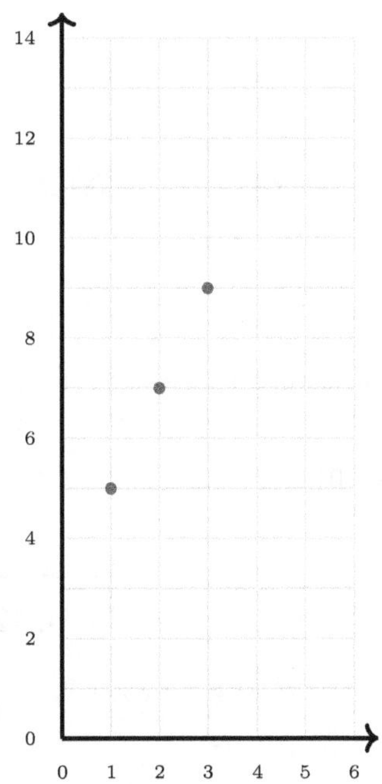

☐ A. (4, 11)
☐ B. (4, 10)
☐ C. (5, 11)
☐ D. (3, 11)

13) Divide: $840 \div 35$

☐ A. 22
☐ B. 24
☐ C. 26
☐ D. 28

14) If the population is 15×10^7, how many people?

☐ A. 15 million
☐ B. 150 million
☐ C. 15 billion
☐ D. 150 thousand

15) Find: $1 \times \frac{5}{9}$.

Record your answer in the space provided.

16) Which phrase matches $8 \times (6 - 2)$?

☐ A. 8 times 6 minus 2
☐ B. 8 times the difference of 6 and 2
☐ C. The difference of 8 times 6 and 2
☐ D. 2 less than 8 times 6

17) Round 12.542 to the nearest tenth.

☐ A. 12.4
☐ B. 13.0
☐ C. 12.6
☐ D. 12.5

18) What is 5.6×1.5?

☐ A. 8.1
☐ B. 8.3
☐ C. 8.4
☐ D. 9.1

19) Multiplying 2.5 by 100 moves the decimal point two places to the right. What is 2.5×100?

☐ A. 25 ☐ C. 2,500
☐ B. 250 ☐ D. 25,000

20) If $2\frac{1}{4} + ? = 5$, what is the missing number?

☐ A. $2\frac{1}{2}$ ☐ C. 3
☐ B. $2\frac{3}{4}$ ☐ D. $3\frac{1}{4}$

21) A baker had $11\frac{3}{4}$ pounds of sugar. He used $6\frac{1}{4}$ pounds for a cake. How much sugar remains?

☐ A. $4\frac{1}{2}$ lb ☐ C. $5\frac{1}{2}$ lb
☐ B. 5 lb ☐ D. 6 lb

22) A square is being placed in a Venn diagram with circles for rectangles, rhombuses, and parallelograms. Which statements are true? *Select all that apply.*

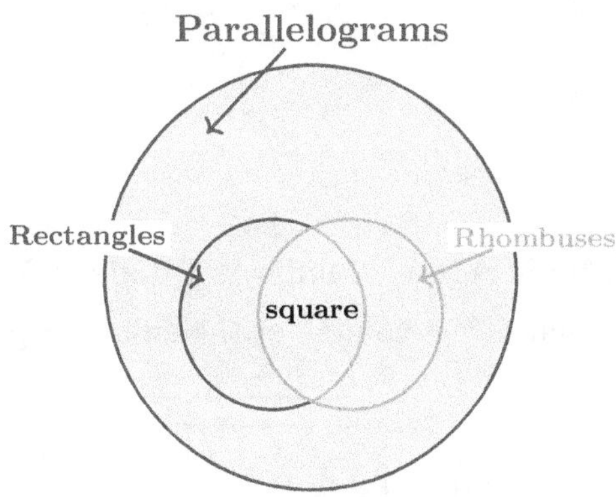

☐ A. It belongs in none of the circles. ☐ C. It belongs in the rhombus circle.
☐ B. It belongs in the circle for rectangles. ☐ D. It belongs in the parallelogram circle.

23) Subtract: $\frac{2}{5} - \frac{1}{10}$

☐ A. $\frac{3}{10}$
☐ B. $\frac{1}{5}$
☐ C. $\frac{2}{5}$
☐ D. $\frac{2}{15}$

24) Which type of quadrilateral listed below always has four right angles?

☐ A. Trapezoid
☐ B. Rhombus
☐ C. Rectangle
☐ D. Parallelogram

25) A snack package weighs 8 ounces. How many such packages equal 1 pound? (1 pound = 16 ounces)

☐ A. 1 package
☐ B. 2 packages
☐ C. 3 packages
☐ D. 4 packages

26) Without calculating, which comparison is correct?

☐ A. $15 \times 8 > 16 \times 8$
☐ B. $24 \times 6 < 24 \times 5$
☐ C. $9 \times 14 = 14 \times 9$
☐ D. $30 \times 3 > 30 \times 4$

27) A rectangular prism with dimensions 3 units × 4 units × 5 units is enlarged so that each dimension is doubled. What is the volume of the enlarged prism?

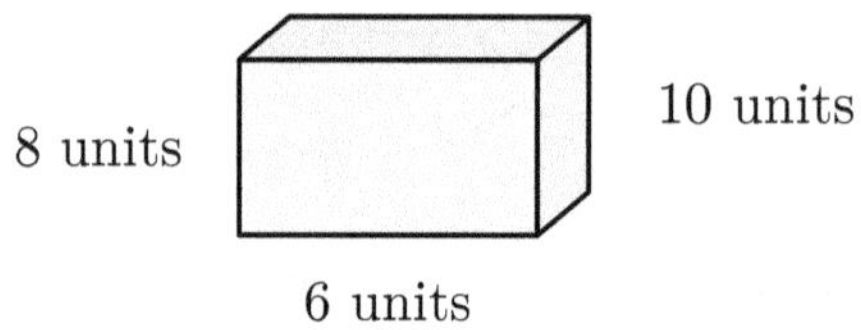

☐ A. 120 cubic units
☐ B. 240 cubic units
☐ C. 480 cubic units
☐ D. 960 cubic units

28) The model shows $\frac{1}{3}$ of a whole split into 6 equal parts. What fraction of the whole is each small part?

$\frac{1}{3}$ split into 6

1 whole split into 3 equal parts

☐ A. $\frac{1}{3}$

☐ B. $\frac{1}{6}$

☐ C. $\frac{1}{18}$

☐ D. $\frac{1}{9}$

29) Complete the subtraction using the place-value chart:

Tens	Ones	Tenths	Hundredths
1	6	8	3
−0	−4	−5	−8

What is the difference?

☐ A. 12.25

☐ B. 12.13

☐ C. 11.03

☐ D. 11.75

30) Pattern A: $1, 2, 3, 4, \ldots$. Pattern B: $5, 10, 15, 20, \ldots$. Which ordered pair represents the 4th terms of Patterns A and B?

Record your answer in the space provided.

31) Find: 135×27.

Record your answer in the space provided.

32) A hundredths grid shows: Grid A has 42 shaded; Grid B has 35 shaded. Find the sum as a decimal.

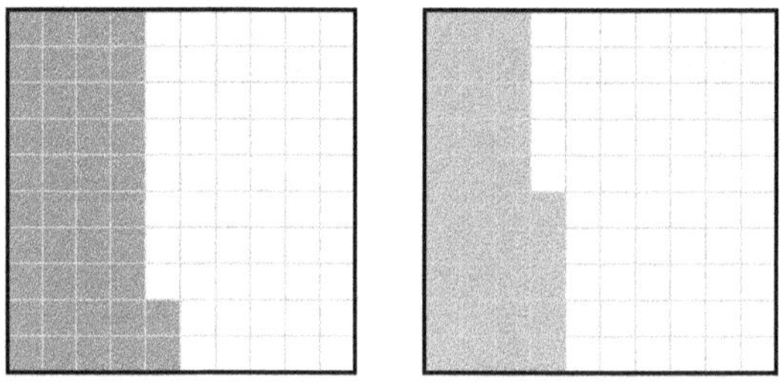

Grid A: 0.42 Grid B: 0.35

What is $0.42 + 0.35$?

☐ A. 0.67
☐ B. 0.97
☐ C. 0.87
☐ D. 0.77

33) The bar model shows 3 groups. Each group has $(2 + 3)$ units. Which expression matches the model?

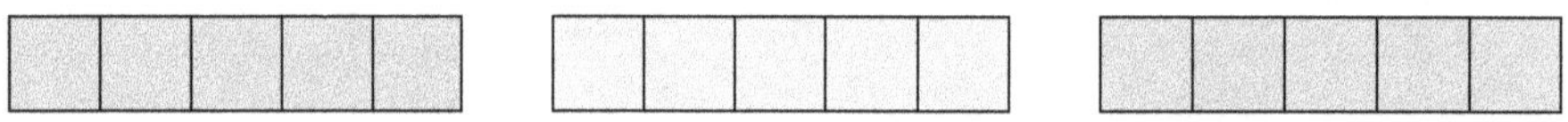

Group 1 (5 units) Group 2 (5 units) Group 3 (5 units)

☐ A. $(2 + 3) + 3$
☐ B. $3 \times (2 + 3)$
☐ C. $3 \times 2 + 3$
☐ D. $(3 + 3) \times 2$

34) What is $\frac{2}{3} \times 6$?

- ☐ A. $\frac{12}{5}$
- ☐ B. 4
- ☐ C. $\frac{2}{18}$
- ☐ D. $2\frac{2}{3}$

35) Plot these four points: $(1, 1)$, $(1, 8)$, $(9, 1)$, $(9, 8)$. What shape do they form?

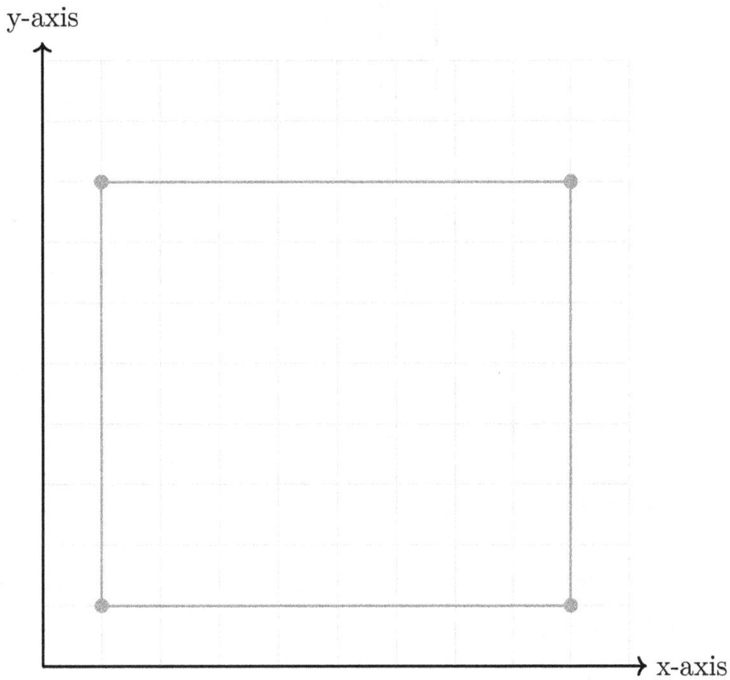

- ☐ A. A triangle
- ☐ B. A circle
- ☐ C. A straight line
- ☐ D. A rectangle

36) What is $4,300 \div 10$?

- ☐ A. 4.3
- ☐ B. 43
- ☐ C. 43,000
- ☐ D. 430

37) A bus trip costs $\$2\frac{1}{2}$ per person. What is the total cost for 5 people?

☐ A. $\$12\frac{1}{2}$
☐ B. $15
☐ C. $\$17\frac{1}{2}$
☐ D. $10

38) Use the area model below to find $\frac{3}{4} \times \frac{1}{2}$.

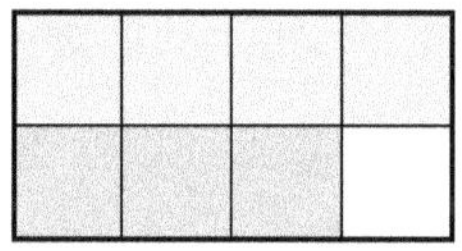

Record your answer in the space provided.

39) Which statement is true about a right triangle?

☐ A. It has all angles less than 90°
☐ B. It has exactly one angle of 90°
☐ C. It has two angles of 90°
☐ D. It has no angles of 90°

40) One twelfth of a garden row is divided into 4 equal parts. Which division equation finds each share?

☐ A. $4 \div \frac{1}{12} = n$
☐ B. $\frac{1}{12} \times 4 = n$
☐ C. $4 + \frac{1}{12} = n$
☐ D. $\frac{1}{12} \div 4 = n$

End of Practice Test

Take a short breath, then check your work with care. Good corrections can teach almost as much as the test itself.

Sketch It Out! ✓

You finished a full test. That takes focus and stamina.
Pictures unlock answers that words hide.

Draw the Problem ★

Maryam Mirzakhani was the first woman to win the Fields Medal, the top math prize. She loved drawing as much as solving. Her notebooks were full of doodles, diagrams, and shapes.
She said her drawings helped her see the math. When numbers were hard, pictures made them easier.
In 5th grade, this works for area, perimeter, fractions, time, and word problems. Sketch it, and the answer often shows up.

Math Mindset Tip: **When stuck, draw. A small sketch reveals the path forward.**

A picture is your shortcut to understanding.
— Math Mindset

Mirzakhani's Amazing Journey ★

Maryam's drawings weren't fancy. They were simple shapes labeled with numbers and arrows.

Try this: on the next word problem, draw a quick picture in the margin. A bar, a number line, a rectangle, a circle. Label what you know.

When the picture is clear, the math becomes clear too.

Mirzakhani's Secret: **Math is visual—draw it and you'll see it.**

Try this on your next practice test. Small, smart habits become big score boosters.

★ Sketch. Label. Solve. ★

Your drawing is your guide to the answer.

Grade 5 Math

Grade 5 Mathematics

6

Questions: 40 **Duration:** No time limit

Calculator Policy: Calculators are not allowed

Grade 5 Mathematics Reference Materials

PERIMETER AND AREA

Perimeter of Rectangle	$P = 2l + 2w$ or $P = 2(l + w)$
Area of Rectangle	$A = l \times w$
Area of Triangle	$A = \frac{1}{2} \times b \times h$
Volume of Rectangular Prism	$V = l \times w \times h$

LENGTH

Customary	**Metric**
1 foot (ft) = 12 inches (in.)	1 meter (m) = 100 centimeters (cm)
1 yard (yd) = 3 feet (ft)	1 centimeter (cm) = 10 millimeters (mm)
1 yard (yd) = 36 inches (in.)	1 kilometer (km) = 1,000 meters (m)

CAPACITY

Customary	**Metric**
1 cup (c) = 8 fluid ounces (fl oz)	1 liter (L) = 1,000 milliliters (mL)
1 pint (pt) = 2 cups (c)	
1 quart (qt) = 2 pints (pt)	
1 gallon (gal) = 4 quarts (qt)	

WEIGHT AND MASS

Customary	**Metric**
1 pound (lb) = 16 ounces (oz)	1 kilogram (kg) = 1,000 grams (g)
	1 gram (g) = 1,000 milligrams (mg)

TIME

1 minute (min) = 60 seconds (sec)	1 week = 7 days
1 hour (hr) = 60 minutes (min)	1 year = 12 months
1 day = 24 hours (hr)	1 year = 52 weeks

1) Which point is highest on the grid?

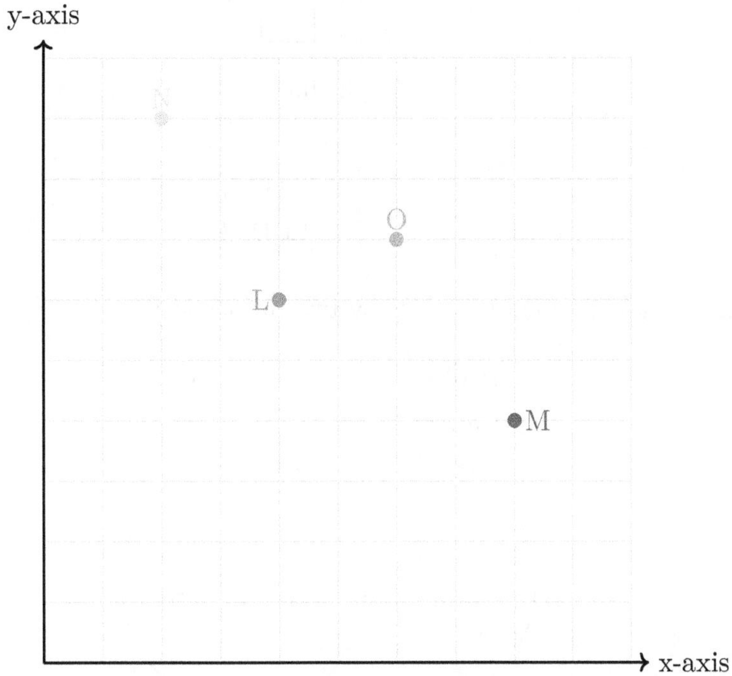

☐ A. L

☐ B. M

☐ C. N

☐ D. O

2)

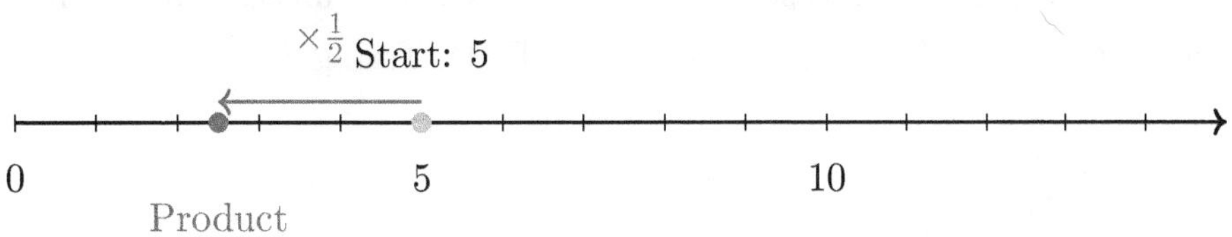

Where does the product land when 5 is scaled by $\frac{1}{2}$?

☐ A. At 1

☐ B. At $2\frac{1}{2}$

☐ C. At 5

☐ D. At 10

3) What is $\frac{1}{8} \div 5$?

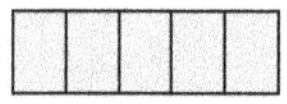

$\frac{1}{8}$ split into 5

- ☐ A. $\frac{5}{8}$
- ☐ B. $\frac{1}{40}$
- ☐ C. $\frac{1}{13}$
- ☐ D. $\frac{1}{3}$

4) A Venn diagram classifies quadrilaterals by two properties:

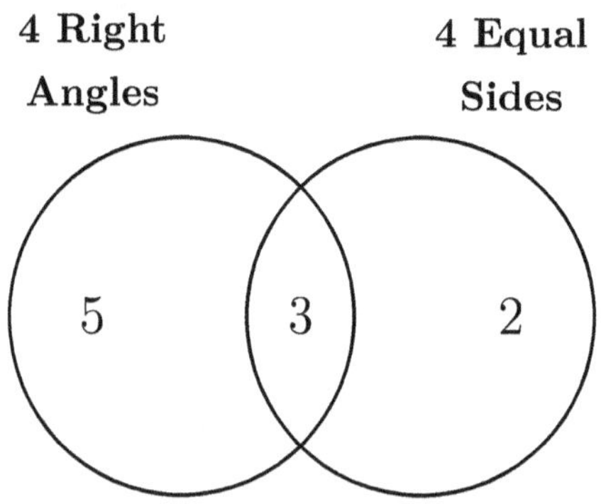

Which type of figure is represented by the number 3?

- ☐ A. Rectangles that are not squares
- ☐ B. Squares
- ☐ C. Rhombuses that are not squares
- ☐ D. Triangles

5) Which statement is true?

- ☐ A. $0.5 \neq 0.50$
- ☐ B. $0.5 < 0.50$
- ☐ C. $0.5 > 0.50$
- ☐ D. $0.5 = 0.50$

6) Write the fraction $\frac{15}{25}$ in simplest form.

Record your answer in the space provided.

7) A point is located 5 blocks east and 3 blocks north from the origin. What are the coordinates of this point?

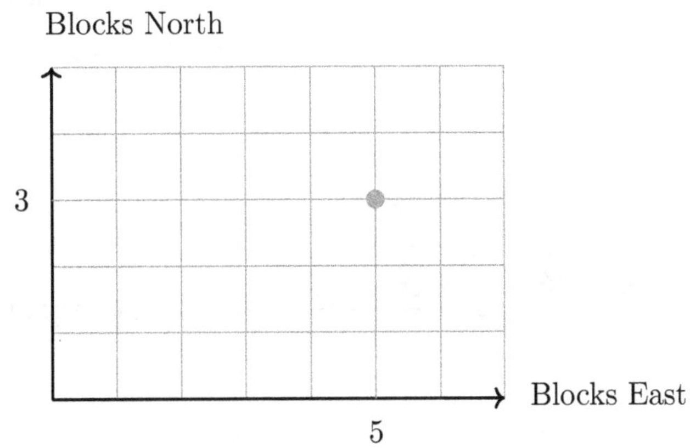

- ☐ A. $(3, 5)$
- ☐ B. $(5, 8)$
- ☐ C. $(8, 3)$
- ☐ D. $(5, 3)$

8) What is the least common denominator for $\frac{5}{12}$ and $\frac{7}{9}$?

- ☐ A. 36
- ☐ B. 21
- ☐ C. 108
- ☐ D. 48

9) Three decimal lengths: 1.5 m, 0.15 m, 0.015 m. Multiply each by 100 (to convert to centimeters). Which result is the largest?

- ☐ A. $1.5 \times 100 = 150$ cm
- ☐ B. $0.15 \times 100 = 15$ cm
- ☐ C. $0.015 \times 100 = 1.5$ cm
- ☐ D. All equal

10) A student incorrectly says: "This shape has 4 equal sides, so it CANNOT be a rectangle." Why is this reasoning WRONG?

- ☐ A. Rectangles must have 4 equal sides.
- ☐ B. Having 4 equal sides does NOT prevent a shape from also being a rectangle.
- ☐ C. 4 equal sides means it is definitely a trapezoid.
- ☐ D. Equal sides and rectangles are unrelated.

11) The line plot shows temperatures (in degrees Celsius) recorded at different times:

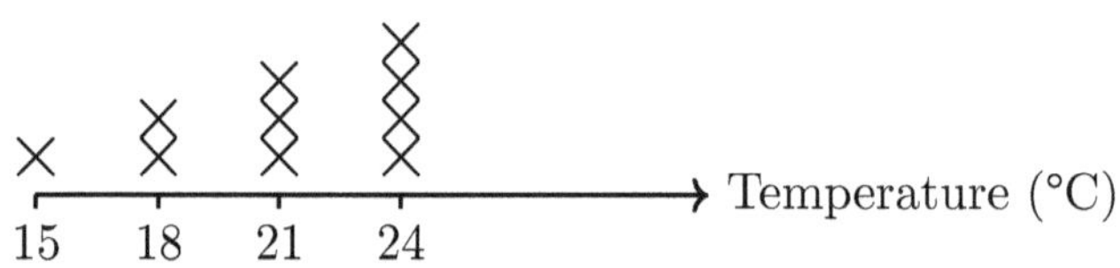

What is the difference between the highest and lowest temperatures recorded?

- ☐ A. 6°C
- ☐ B. 8°C
- ☐ C. 9°C
- ☐ D. 10°C

12) A recipe calls for 1.25 kilograms of sugar to make 20 servings. How much sugar is needed to make 80 servings?

- ☐ A. 4.75 kg
- ☐ B. 5.00 kg
- ☐ C. 5.25 kg
- ☐ D. 5.50 kg

13) Error analysis: Jon reads 2.04 as “two and four tenths”. What is the correct reading?

☐ A. Two and four hundredths

☐ B. Two point four

☐ C. Two and four tenths

☐ D. Two and forty tenths

14) Find: $\frac{7}{8} \times \frac{2}{3}$.

Record your answer in the space provided.

15) A point that is 9 units right of the origin and 4 units up from the origin has coordinates:

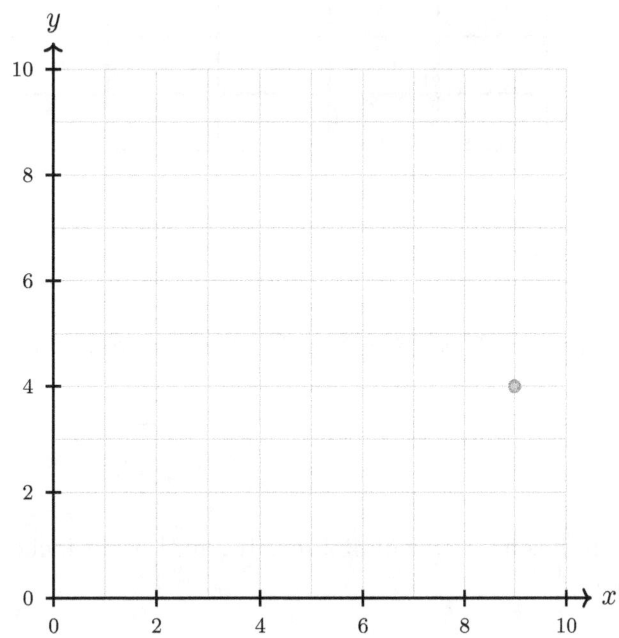

☐ A. $(4, 9)$

☐ B. $(4, 4)$

☐ C. $(9, 9)$

☐ D. $(9, 4)$

16)

73.5 grams

↓

Divide by 10

?

What is $73.5 \div 10$?

☐ A. 0.735 grams

☐ B. 7.35 grams

☐ C. 735 grams

☐ D. 7350 grams

17) A bookstore sells $\frac{1}{5}$ of its book inventory on Monday and $\frac{2}{10}$ on Tuesday. What fraction of the inventory is sold in all?

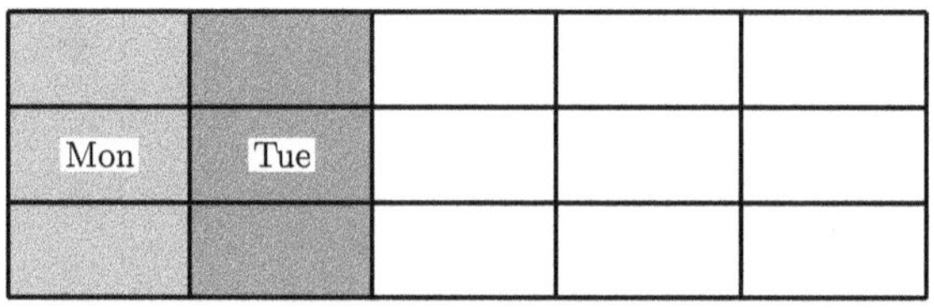

☐ A. $\frac{3}{10}$

☐ B. $\frac{3}{15}$

☐ C. $\frac{4}{10}$

☐ D. $\frac{5}{10}$

18) Which products can be modeled by a $\frac{3}{4}$-by-$\frac{1}{2}$ rectangle? *Select all that apply.*

☐ A. $\frac{3}{4} \times \frac{1}{2}$

☐ B. $\frac{1}{2} \times \frac{3}{4}$

☐ C. $\frac{3}{4} + \frac{1}{2}$

☐ D. $\frac{3}{8} \times 2$

19) A rectangular prism has a volume of 432 in^3. If length is 18 inches and height is 8 inches, what is the width?

☐ A. 2 inches

☐ B. 3 inches

☐ C. 4 inches

☐ D. 5 inches

20) A rectangular prism has dimensions 13 m, 2 m, and 4 m. What is its volume?

☐ A. 104 m^3
☐ B. 19 m^3
☐ C. 52 m^3
☐ D. 26 m^3

21) A rectangular prism has dimensions 7 units, 2 units, and 1 unit. How many unit cubes fill it?

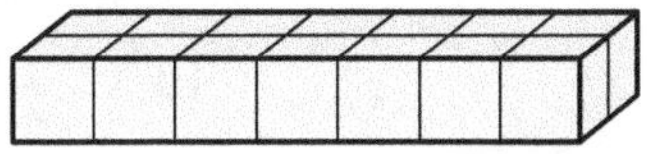

☐ A. 7 unit cubes
☐ B. 10 unit cubes
☐ C. 14 unit cubes
☐ D. 9 unit cubes

22) Find $\frac{1}{3}$ of 30.

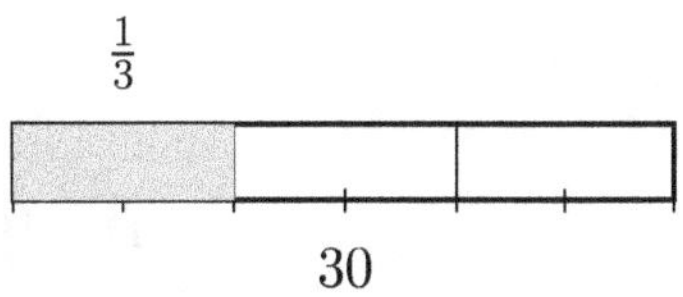

☐ A. 10
☐ B. 15
☐ C. 20
☐ D. 30

23) A carpenter uses $\frac{2}{5}$ yard of wood for one project and $\frac{3}{10}$ yard for another. How much wood total?

☐ A. $\frac{5}{15}$ yard
☐ B. $\frac{3}{4}$ yard
☐ C. $\frac{12}{10}$ yard
☐ D. $\frac{7}{10}$ yard

24) Pattern table shows input-output pairs: $(1, 7), (2, 14), (3, 21), (4, 28)$. Which rule applies?

☐ A. Add 6 to the input.
☐ B. Multiply the input by 7.
☐ C. Multiply the input by itself, then add 6.
☐ D. Multiply the input by 5, then add 2.

25) Evaluate: $(9 - 3) \times (4 + 2) \div 4$

☐ A. 6
☐ B. 15
☐ C. 12
☐ D. 9

26) What is $14 \div \frac{1}{3}$?

☐ A. 28
☐ B. 35
☐ C. 42
☐ D. 48

27) Which expanded form correctly represents 7.346?

☐ A. $7 + 0.3 + 0.04 + 0.006$
☐ B. $7 + 3 + 4 + 6$
☐ C. $70 + 3 + 0.4 + 0.06$
☐ D. $7 + 0.03 + 0.04 + 0.006$

28) What is 225×4?

☐ A. 880
☐ B. 890
☐ C. 900
☐ D. 910

29) What is the total volume of a composite solid made from non-overlapping prisms that measure 6 cm by 4 cm by 3 cm and 5 cm by 4 cm by 3 cm?

Record your answer in the space provided.

30) Pattern W starts at 6 and increases by 2. Pattern X starts at 1 and increases by 1. At step 4 in the table, what is the sum of the two terms?

Step	W	X
1	6	1
2	8	2
3	10	3
4	?	?

☐ A. 15
☐ B. 18
☐ C. 17
☐ D. 16

31) The line plot shows the number of books read during summer break:

Books Read Over Summer

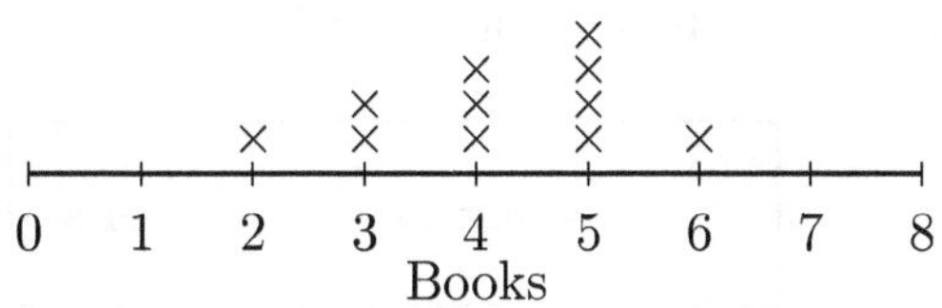

How many students read at least 4 books?

☐ A. 5
☐ B. 6
☐ C. 7
☐ D. 8

32) Estimate: $9\frac{2}{3} - 6\frac{8}{9}$.

☐ A. 2
☐ B. 5
☐ C. 4
☐ D. 3

33) What result completes the table?

Expression	Result
5 × 100	500
5 × 1000	?

☐ A. 500
☐ B. 5000
☐ C. 50000
☐ D. 100

34) How many $\frac{1}{6}$-hour music lessons can fit into 2 hours?

☐ A. 6 lessons
☐ B. 8 lessons
☐ C. 10 lessons
☐ D. 12 lessons

35) Place-value diagram: When we multiply 40 by 50, we can think of it as 4 × 10 and 5 × 10. How many groups of 10 are in the product 2,000?

$4 \times 5 = 20$	**tens**

tens	Product = 2,000

☐ A. 20 groups of 10
☐ B. 100 groups of 10
☐ C. 2,000 groups of 10
☐ D. 200 groups of 10

36) Order from smallest to largest: 10^2, 2×10^3, 10^4, 3×10^2.

Expression	Value
10^2	100
2×10^3	2000
10^4	10000
3×10^2	300

☐ A. $10^2, 3 \times 10^2, 2 \times 10^3, 10^4$

☐ B. $3 \times 10^2, 10^2, 2 \times 10^3, 10^4$

☐ C. $10^2, 2 \times 10^3, 3 \times 10^2, 10^4$

☐ D. $10^4, 2 \times 10^3, 10^2, 3 \times 10^2$

37) A farmer has 1,232 pounds of grain to divide equally among 16 animals. How many pounds per animal?

☐ A. 77

☐ B. 75

☐ C. 73

☐ D. 71

38) A solid figure has volume 30 cubic units. If it is 5 cubes long and 3 cubes wide, how tall is it?

Record your answer in the space provided.

39) A garden bed is 9 feet long, 4 feet wide, and 2 feet deep. What is the volume of soil it can hold?

Record your answer in the space provided.

40) Which is greater: $\frac{3}{5}$ or $\frac{2}{3}$? By how much?

- ☐ A. $\frac{3}{5}$ by $\frac{1}{15}$
- ☐ B. $\frac{3}{5}$ by $\frac{1}{2}$
- ☐ C. Equal
- ☐ D. $\frac{2}{3}$ by $\frac{1}{15}$

End of Practice Test

Take a short breath, then check your work with care. Good corrections can teach almost as much as the test itself.

Math Teamwork!

You finished a full test. That takes focus and stamina.

Talking through math makes thinking sharper.

Share Ideas, Learn Faster

Akio loved math, but his favorite part was talking about it. When a problem stumped him, he explained it out loud to his little sister, his stuffed bear, or even his pencil.

Saying the problem out loud forced him to slow down. Often, the answer appeared while he was still talking.

On a test, you can't talk out loud, but you can "talk" in your head. Read the problem to yourself in your own words. Then solve.

Math Mindset Tip: **Explain a problem to yourself first. Your words are your map.**

If you can explain it, you can solve it.

— Math Mindset

Akio's Amazing Journey ★

Akio noticed that hearing his own voice unstuck his brain. He stopped worrying about "sounding smart" and started just thinking out loud.

On a tricky test problem, ask yourself silently: "What is this asking? What do I know? What's missing?" Answer in your own words. The answer often appears.

It works because explaining is thinking. The clearer you explain, the clearer you think.

Akio's Secret: **Explain first. Solve second.**

Try this on your next practice test. Small, smart habits become big score boosters.

★ Talk it through. Then solve it through. ★

Your own words are your best math tool.

Grade 5 Math

Grade 5 Mathematics

7

Questions: 40 **Duration:** No time limit

Calculator Policy: Calculators are not allowed

Grade 5 Mathematics Reference Materials

PERIMETER AND AREA

Perimeter of Rectangle	$P = 2l + 2w$ or $P = 2(l + w)$
Area of Rectangle	$A = l \times w$
Area of Triangle	$A = \frac{1}{2} \times b \times h$
Volume of Rectangular Prism	$V = l \times w \times h$

LENGTH

Customary	**Metric**
1 foot (ft) = 12 inches (in.)	1 meter (m) = 100 centimeters (cm)
1 yard (yd) = 3 feet (ft)	1 centimeter (cm) = 10 millimeters (mm)
1 yard (yd) = 36 inches (in.)	1 kilometer (km) = 1,000 meters (m)

CAPACITY

Customary	**Metric**
1 cup (c) = 8 fluid ounces (fl oz)	1 liter (L) = 1,000 milliliters (mL)
1 pint (pt) = 2 cups (c)	
1 quart (qt) = 2 pints (pt)	
1 gallon (gal) = 4 quarts (qt)	

WEIGHT AND MASS

Customary	**Metric**
1 pound (lb) = 16 ounces (oz)	1 kilogram (kg) = 1,000 grams (g)
	1 gram (g) = 1,000 milligrams (mg)

TIME

1 minute (min) = 60 seconds (sec)	1 week = 7 days
1 hour (hr) = 60 minutes (min)	1 year = 12 months
1 day = 24 hours (hr)	1 year = 52 weeks

1) Compare: $4.2 \times 5 \square 4.2 \times 5.1$

☐ A. $>$
☐ B. $<$
☐ C. $=$
☐ D. Cannot tell

2) A rope is 3 m long. It is cut into pieces of 25 cm each. How many pieces?

Record your answer in the space provided.

3) A large jug holds 2 gallons. How many cups can be filled from this jug? (1 gallon = 16 cups)

☐ A. 32 cups
☐ B. 20 cups
☐ C. 48 cups
☐ D. 16 cups

4) Add: $2\frac{1}{6} + 4\frac{5}{6}$

☐ A. $6\frac{1}{3}$
☐ B. 7
☐ C. $6\frac{5}{6}$
☐ D. $7\frac{1}{6}$

5) Which rule describes the relationship in the ordered pairs (1, 3), (2, 5), (3, 7)?

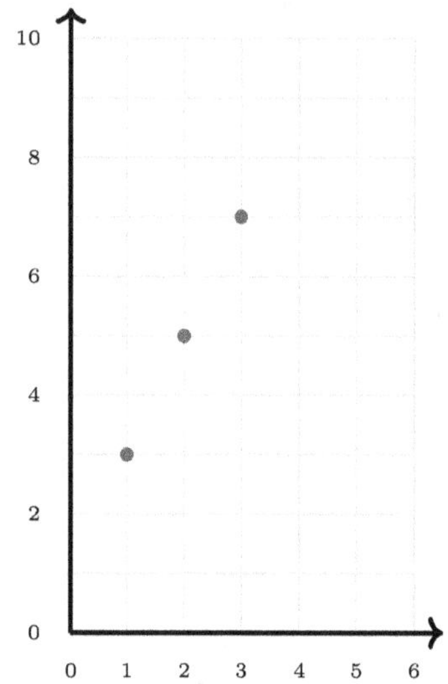

☐ A. Add 1 to the first coordinate

☐ B. Double the first coordinate, then add 1

☐ C. Triple the first coordinate

☐ D. Add 3 to the first coordinate

6) Which model correctly shows 0.6×4?

Option A: Four groups of 0.6

Option B: Shaded 4 out of 10

☐ A. Option A

☐ B. Option B

☐ C. Neither model

☐ D. Both models

7) Convert: 750 cm = ? m.

Record your answer in the space provided.

8) Which expression represents "3 times as many as the sum of 10 and 7"?

☐ A. $3 + 10 + 7$
☐ B. $(3 \times 10) + 7$
☐ C. $10 + 7 \times 3$
☐ D. $3 \times (10 + 7)$

9) A storage locker has a base that is 10 ft by 6 ft. If the volume is 360 ft^3, how tall is the locker?

☐ A. 12 ft
☐ B. 8 ft
☐ C. 10 ft
☐ D. 6 ft

10) The table shows a pattern. What is the missing value?

Input	Output
1	7
2	14
3	21
4	?

☐ A. 24
☐ B. 28
☐ C. 30
☐ D. 32

11) Round 2.48 to the nearest tenth. Use the number line to help.

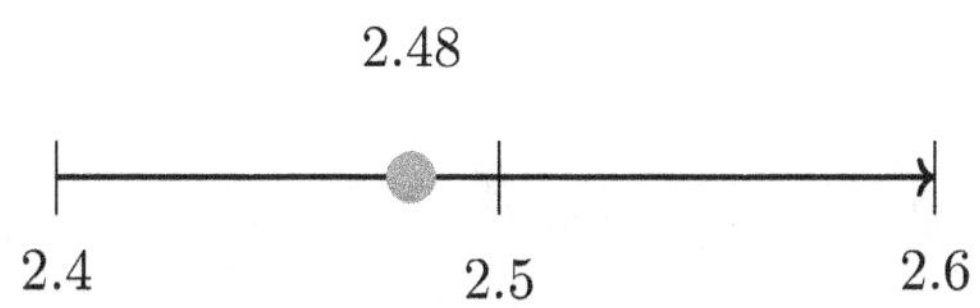

☐ A. 2.4
☐ B. 2.48
☐ C. 2.6
☐ D. 2.5

12) Which fraction is NOT equivalent to $\frac{1}{3}$?

☐ A. $\frac{2}{6}$
☐ B. $\frac{3}{9}$
☐ C. $\frac{4}{12}$
☐ D. $\frac{5}{16}$

13) Multiply: $\frac{1}{4} \times \frac{1}{5}$

☐ A. $\frac{1}{9}$
☐ B. $\frac{2}{9}$
☐ C. $\frac{1}{20}$
☐ D. $\frac{1}{1}$

14) The model shows 3 wholes, with each whole cut into pieces of size $\frac{1}{3}$. How many pieces of size $\frac{1}{3}$ are there in all?

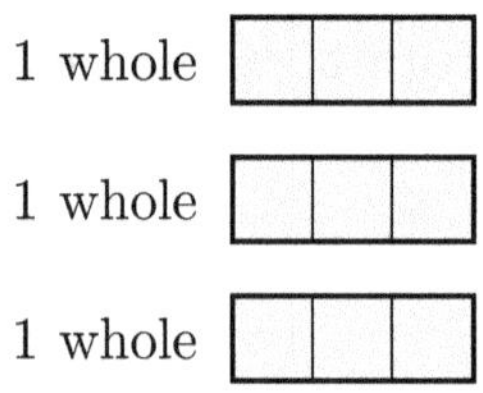

3 wholes, each cut into pieces of size $\frac{1}{3}$

☐ A. 6
☐ B. 3
☐ C. 12
☐ D. 9

15) Find the difference: $6\frac{1}{4} - 2\frac{5}{8}$.

Record your answer in the space provided.

16) A student calculates the volume of a box using only the length and width, forgetting to multiply by the height. The length is 9 cm, the width is 5 cm, and the height is 4 cm. What error was made?

☐ A. Calculated $9 + 5 + 4 = 18$ (perimeter formula)

☐ B. Calculated $9 + 5 = 14$ (used only two dimensions)

☐ C. Calculated $9 \times 5 \times 4 = 180$ (correct answer)

☐ D. Calculated $9 \times 5 = 45$ (missing height multiplication)

17) An area model shows a grid with 10 columns and 6 rows (60 squares total). The blue shading covers 3 columns, and the red shading covers 4 rows. How many squares are in the double-shaded overlap, and what fraction is that?

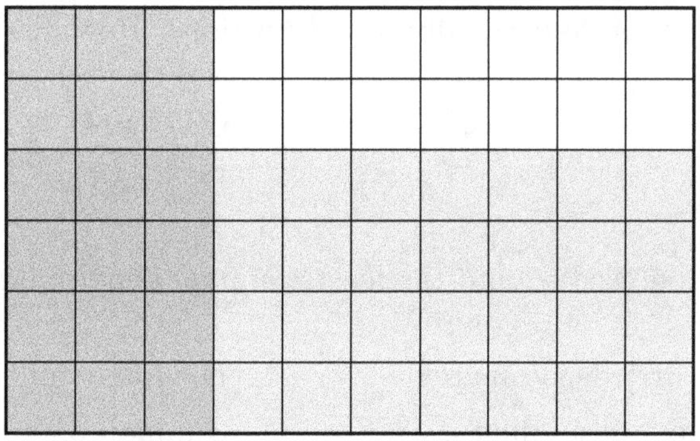

☐ A. 12 squares, $\frac{12}{60}$

☐ B. 7 squares, $\frac{7}{60}$

☐ C. 8 squares, $\frac{8}{60}$

☐ D. 10 squares, $\frac{10}{60}$

18) Which expressions match the phrase "three times the sum of 5 and 2"? *Select all that apply.*

☐ A. $3 \times (5 + 2)$

☐ B. $3 \times 5 + 2$

☐ C. $(5 + 2) \times 3$

☐ D. $3 + 5 \times 2$

19) A student has 30 marbles. He gives away $\frac{3}{5}$ of them to a friend. How many marbles does he give away?

☐ A. 6 marbles
☐ B. 12 marbles
☐ C. 18 marbles
☐ D. 25 marbles

20) A composite science fair model is made from two non-overlapping rectangular prisms. Prism A is 7 meters long, 4 meters wide, and 2 meters tall. Prism B is 6 meters long, 2 meters wide, and 1 meter tall. What is the total volume?

☐ A. 56 cubic meters
☐ B. 12 cubic meters
☐ C. 96 cubic meters
☐ D. 68 cubic meters

21) A baker divides $\frac{1}{2}$ cup of flour equally into 4 portions. How much flour is in each portion?

☐ A. $\frac{1}{2}$ cup
☐ B. $\frac{1}{6}$ cup
☐ C. $\frac{4}{2}$ cups
☐ D. $\frac{1}{8}$ cup

22) Which method can be used to find the least common denominator?

☐ A. Use only the first denominator
☐ B. Find the largest denominator
☐ C. Add the denominators
☐ D. List multiples and find the first common one

23) The line plot shows the heights of plants in Mrs. Garcia's garden:

Plant Heights in Garden

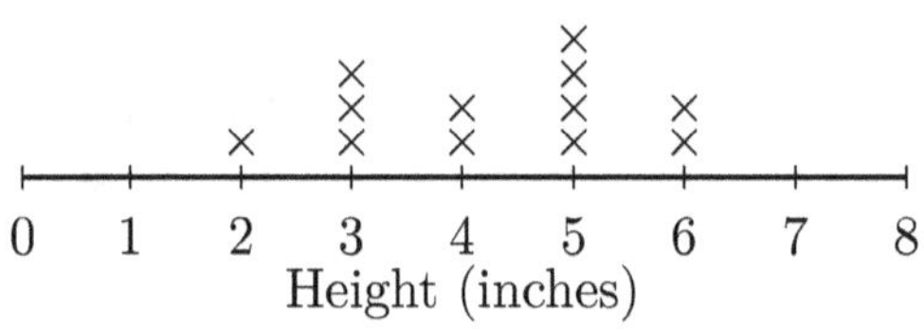

What is the most common plant height?

☐ A. 3 inches
☐ B. 4 inches
☐ C. 5 inches
☐ D. 6 inches

24) Which pair of fractions sums to closest to $\frac{1}{2}$?

☐ A. $\frac{1}{3} + \frac{1}{7}$
☐ B. $\frac{1}{4} + \frac{1}{4}$
☐ C. $\frac{1}{5} + \frac{1}{5}$
☐ D. $\frac{2}{7} + \frac{1}{8}$

25) A Venn diagram shows squares inside rectangles. There are 6 rectangles that are not squares and 4 squares. How many rectangles are shown in all?

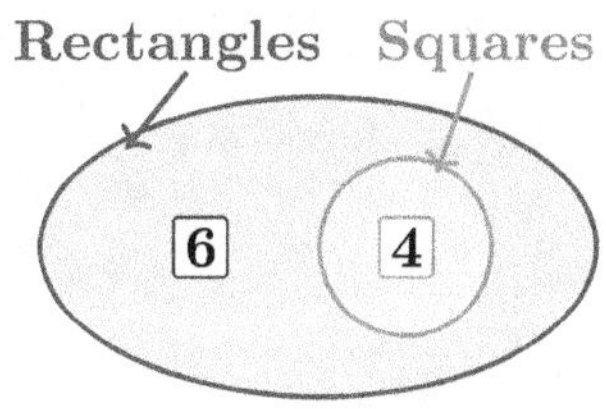

☐ A. 4
☐ B. 6
☐ C. 14
☐ D. 10

26) A scientist records 0.023 grams. If the scale multiplies this by 10^2, what is the result?

☐ A. 0.23 g
☐ B. 2.3 g
☐ C. 23 g
☐ D. 230 g

27) Which point is located at $(2, 8)$ on this coordinate plane?

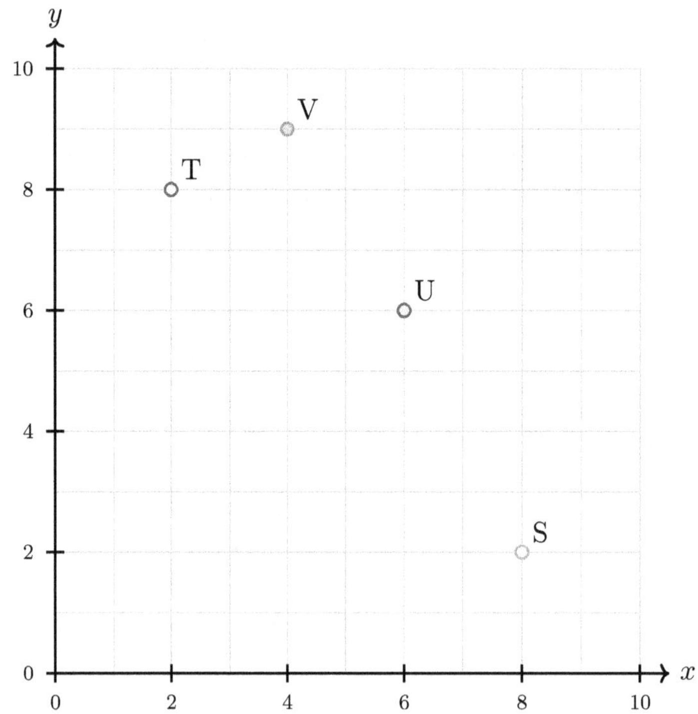

☐ A. Point S
☐ B. Point T
☐ C. Point U
☐ D. Point V

28) Pattern E: 2, 4, 6, 8. Pattern F: 6, 12, 18, 24. What is the relationship?

E	F
2	6
4	12
6	18
8	24

☐ A. $F = E + 5$
☐ B. $F = E \times 3$
☐ C. $F = E + 7$
☐ D. $F = E - 2$

29) A rectangular picture frame is $\frac{7}{8}$ meter tall and $\frac{3}{5}$ meter wide. What is the area of the frame?

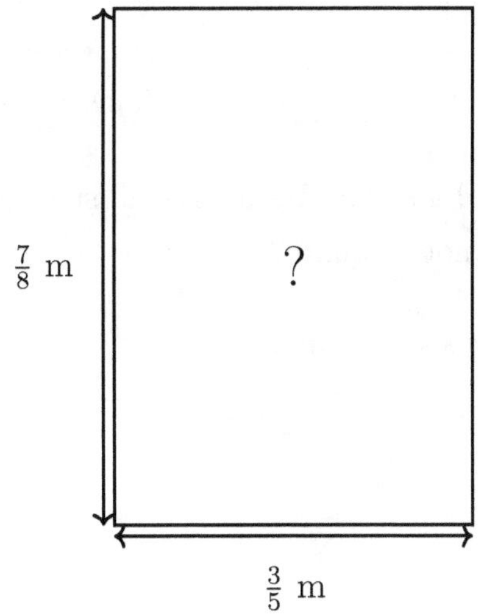

☐ A. $\frac{21}{40}$ m^2

☐ B. $\frac{10}{13}$ m^2

☐ C. $\frac{1}{2}$ m^2

☐ D. 1 m^2

30) How many one-third pizzas fit in 2 whole pizzas?

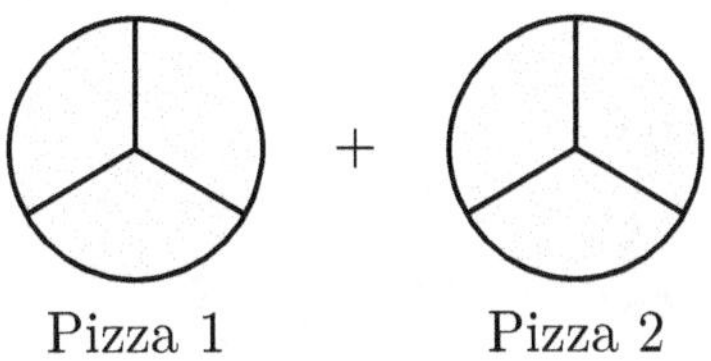

Each whole pizza is split into thirds

☐ A. 8

☐ B. 2

☐ C. 3

☐ D. 6

31) Complete the statement: If you multiply 10 by a fraction less than 1, the product will be ______ 10.

☐ A. equal to
☐ B. greater than
☐ C. less than
☐ D. cannot compare to

32) An equilateral triangle and a square both have all sides equal. What attribute shows that the equilateral triangle is not a square?

Record your answer in the space provided.

33) A fruit stand sells apples at \$0.85 per pound. If a customer buys 6.5 pounds, what is the cost to the nearest cent?

☐ A. \$5.25
☐ B. \$5.50
☐ C. \$5.53
☐ D. \$6.00

34) Find the product: $0.07 \times 1{,}000$.

Record your answer in the space provided.

35) Error analysis: Sarah writes $\frac{6}{10}$ as 0.06 instead of 0.6. Identify her mistake.

☐ A. Sarah placed the digit 6 in the hundredths place instead of the tenths place.

☐ B. Sarah should have written it as a mixed number.

☐ C. $\frac{6}{10}$ cannot be written as a decimal.

☐ D. Sarah forgot to add a zero.

36) What is $\frac{1}{6} \times 5$?

☐ A. $\frac{5}{1}$ ☐ C. $\frac{6}{5}$

☐ B. $\frac{5}{6}$ ☐ D. $\frac{1}{30}$

37) Using powers of 10, what is $\dfrac{6,800}{10^3}$?

☐ A. 68 ☐ C. 6,800

☐ B. 680 ☐ D. 6.8

38) A teacher has 1 pound of modeling clay. Each table group needs $\frac{1}{2}$ pound. How many table groups can receive clay?

☐ A. 2 groups ☐ C. 4 groups

☐ B. 3 groups ☐ D. 6 groups

39) Multiply: $2\frac{1}{3} \times 3$

☐ A. 8 ☐ C. 6

☐ B. 9 ☐ D. 7

40) Evaluate: $9 + 8 \div 2 - 3$

☐ A. 5 ☐ C. 10

☐ B. 7 ☐ D. 14

End of Practice Test

Take a short breath, then check your work with care. Good corrections can teach almost as much as the test itself.

Careful Counter! ✓

You finished a full test. That takes focus and stamina.
Counting twice is faster than fixing one wrong answer.

Count Twice, Move Once ★

Priya had a goal: zero counting mistakes. She used a finger when she counted shapes, dots, or items in a list. Then she counted again to be sure.

It felt slow at first, but her scores jumped. "Two seconds to count again" turned into "two more questions correct."

On 5th grade tests, careful counting matters for problems with charts, graphs, money, and equal groups.

Math Mindset Tip: **Count twice. Move once. That's the safest speed.**

Slow counting is the fastest path to correct counting.
— *Math Mindset*

Priya's Amazing Journey ★

Priya didn't trust her first count. Not because she wasn't smart, but because counting is easy to slip on.

Imagine counting 17 items in a chart and accidentally skipping one. You'd have 16. Then your answer is one off. A second careful count catches it.

Try the "count twice" habit on your next test. It's free, it's easy, and it pays off.

Priya's Secret: **Trust your second count more than your first.**

Try this on your next practice test. Small, smart habits become big score boosters.

★ **Count twice. Smile once.** ★

Careful counters become confident solvers.

Grade 5 Math

Grade 5 Mathematics

8

Questions: 40 **Duration:** No time limit

Calculator Policy: Calculators are not allowed

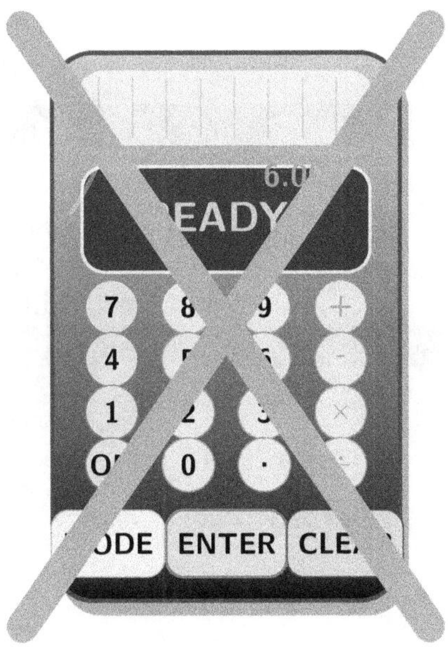

Grade 5 Mathematics Reference Materials

PERIMETER AND AREA

Perimeter of Rectangle	$P = 2l + 2w$ or $P = 2(l + w)$
Area of Rectangle	$A = l \times w$
Area of Triangle	$A = \frac{1}{2} \times b \times h$
Volume of Rectangular Prism	$V = l \times w \times h$

LENGTH

Customary	Metric
1 foot (ft) = 12 inches (in.)	1 meter (m) = 100 centimeters (cm)
1 yard (yd) = 3 feet (ft)	1 centimeter (cm) = 10 millimeters (mm)
1 yard (yd) = 36 inches (in.)	1 kilometer (km) = 1,000 meters (m)

CAPACITY

Customary	Metric
1 cup (c) = 8 fluid ounces (fl oz)	1 liter (L) = 1,000 milliliters (mL)
1 pint (pt) = 2 cups (c)	
1 quart (qt) = 2 pints (pt)	
1 gallon (gal) = 4 quarts (qt)	

WEIGHT AND MASS

Customary	Metric
1 pound (lb) = 16 ounces (oz)	1 kilogram (kg) = 1,000 grams (g)
	1 gram (g) = 1,000 milligrams (mg)

TIME

1 minute (min) = 60 seconds (sec)	1 week = 7 days
1 hour (hr) = 60 minutes (min)	1 year = 12 months
1 day = 24 hours (hr)	1 year = 52 weeks

1) Use the rule shown in the arrow diagram to find which input gives 13.

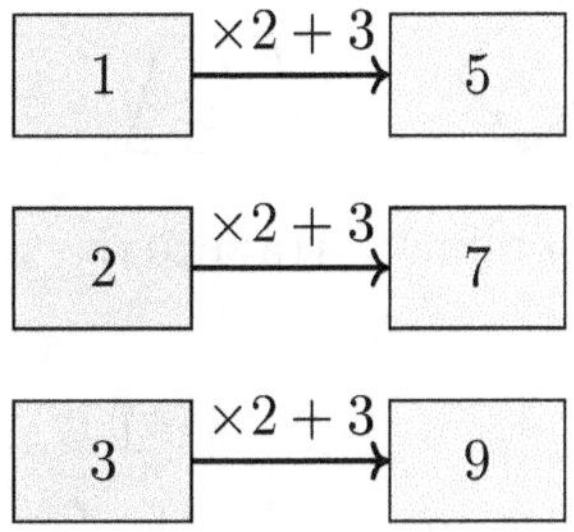

Which input would give an output of 13?

☐ A. 4
☐ B. 5
☐ C. 7
☐ D. 8

2) A triangle has one angle of 90 degrees and sides marked as all different. What type is it?

☐ A. Acute scalene
☐ B. Acute isosceles
☐ C. Obtuse isosceles
☐ D. Right scalene

3) A prism has volume 144 cm^3, length 6 cm, and height 4 cm. Find its width.

Record your answer in the space provided.

4) Which expression is "half of the sum of 12 and 8"?

☐ A. $\frac{1}{2} \times 12 + 8$
☐ B. $\frac{12+8}{2}$
☐ C. $12 + \frac{8}{2}$
☐ D. $\frac{12}{2} + 8$

5) Which statement is false?

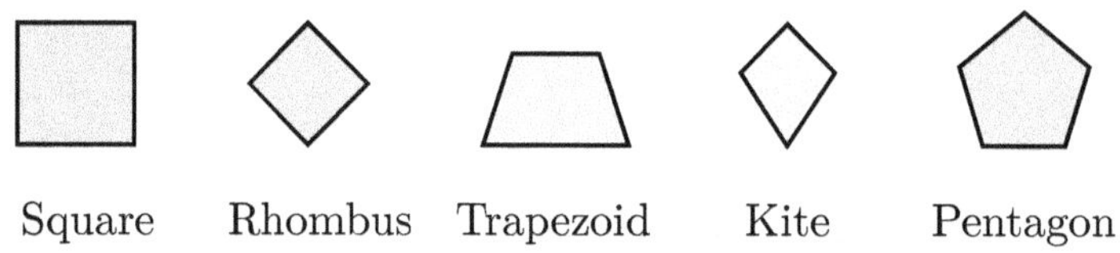

☐ A. A square is a rhombus.

☐ B. A rhombus is a parallelogram.

☐ C. A pentagon is a quadrilateral.

☐ D. A kite has 2 pairs of equal sides.

6) Storage unit: base area 28 ft^2, height 11 ft. Volume =?

☐ A. 308 ft^3

☐ B. 39 ft^3

☐ C. 17 ft^3

☐ D. 280 ft^3

7) Find: $6.7 \div 10^2$.

Record your answer in the space provided.

8) A delivery service maps deliveries on a grid. One delivery is at $(3, 4)$ and another is at $(3, 9)$. How far apart are these two delivery locations?

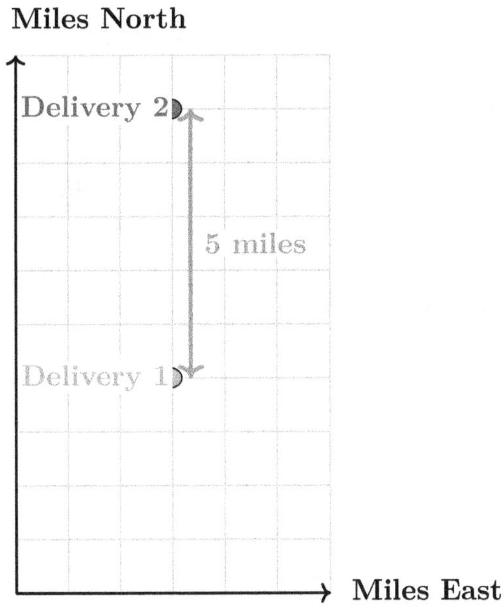

☐ A. 3 miles
☐ B. 4 miles
☐ C. 5 miles
☐ D. 9 miles

9) If all sides of a parallelogram are equal, what is the most specific name?

☐ A. Quadrilateral
☐ B. Parallelogram
☐ C. Rhombus
☐ D. Rectangle

10) Which subtraction problem requires borrowing?

A	B	C	D
6.75 − 2.31	5.82 − 2.56	8.42 − 1.21	7.65 − 3.22

☐ A. A
☐ B. B
☐ C. C
☐ D. D

11) Find the sum and express as a mixed number: $\frac{5}{6}+\frac{3}{4}$

☐ A. $\frac{8}{10}$
☐ B. $\frac{19}{10}$
☐ C. $1\frac{7}{12}$
☐ D. $\frac{9}{12}$

12) Complete: $3.2\times ?=320$.

☐ A. 10
☐ B. 10,000
☐ C. 1,000
☐ D. 100

13) The line plot shows the lengths (in inches) of ribbons collected by the art club:

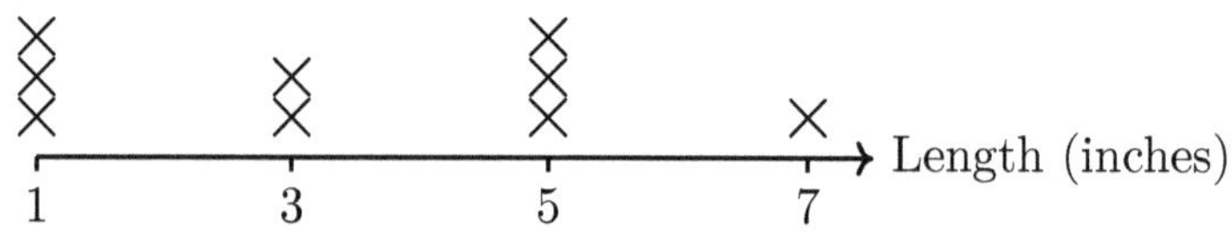

If the total ribbon length is shared equally among 4 posters, how much ribbon goes on each poster?

☐ A. $7\frac{1}{4}$ inches
☐ B. $7\frac{1}{2}$ inches
☐ C. $7\frac{3}{4}$ inches
☐ D. 8 inches

14) Which pair has two expressions that both equal 5000?

☐ A. 40×10 and 4×100
☐ B. 40×10 and 4×1000
☐ C. 50×100 and 500×10
☐ D. 30×1000 and 3×10000

15) A fence is 72 feet long. Posts are placed every 8 feet. How many posts are needed if posts go at the beginning and end?

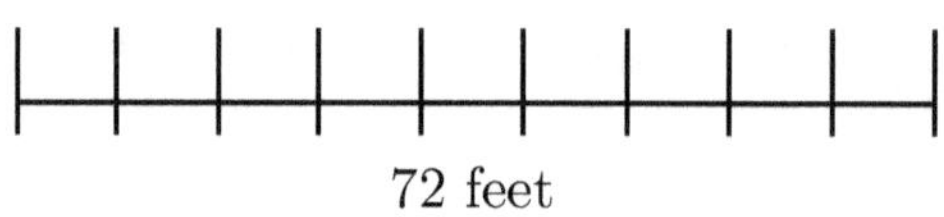

☐ A. 9 posts
☐ B. 8 posts
☐ C. 10 posts
☐ D. 11 posts

16) A rectangular prism has a volume of 500 cm^3. If the length is 25 cm and the width is 5 cm, what is the height?

☐ A. 2 cm
☐ B. 3 cm
☐ C. 4 cm
☐ D. 5 cm

17) A rectangular prism has a volume of 24 cubic units. Which dimensions could create this volume?

Rectangular prism

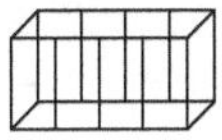

☐ A. Length 2, width 3, height 3
☐ B. Length 2, width 4, height 3
☐ C. Length 2, width 2, height 5
☐ D. Length 3, width 3, height 2

18) How many trailing zeros are in the product 60×700?

☐ A. 2
☐ B. 3
☐ C. 4
☐ D. 5

19) A recipe needs $2\frac{1}{3}$ cups of flour. Sami used $1\frac{1}{2}$ cups. Which statements are true? *Select all that apply.*

☐ A. She still needs $\frac{5}{6}$ cup.
☐ B. She still needs less than 1 cup.
☐ C. She still needs $1\frac{1}{6}$ cups.
☐ D. She has already used more than the recipe calls for.

20) Estimate the product 511×9 by rounding 511 to the nearest hundred.

☐ A. 4,000
☐ B. 4,500
☐ C. 5,000
☐ D. 5,500

21) How many unit cubes fit inside a $2 \times 4 \times 5$ rectangular prism?

Record your answer in the space provided.

22) Number line showing three points. Use the plotted decimals to answer.

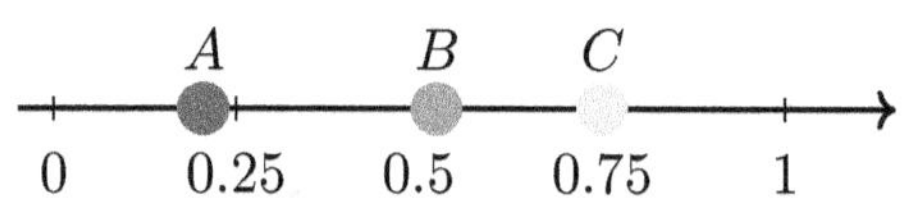

If point A is 0.205, point B is 0.525, point C is 0.75, which is closest to 0.5?

☐ A. Point A
☐ B. Point B
☐ C. Point C
☐ D. Cannot tell

23) The output equals input × input. What ordered pair has input 5?

☐ A. $(5, 10)$
☐ B. $(5, 15)$
☐ C. $(5, 20)$
☐ D. $(5, 25)$

24) Evaluate: $2 \times \{3 + [4 \times (5 - 2)]\}$

☐ A. 24
☐ B. 30
☐ C. 36
☐ D. 42

25) A place-value chart shows a mystery number. Use the chart to identify it.

Ones	Tenths	Hundredths	Thousandths
9	4	2	8

Express this in expanded form.

☐ A. $9 + 4 + 2 + 8$
☐ B. $9 + 0.4 + 0.02 + 0.008$
☐ C. $90 + 4 + 0.2 + 0.008$
☐ D. $9 + 0.04 + 0.002 + 0.008$

26) Find the missing addend: $2.45 + ? = 5.72$

☐ A. 3.27
☐ B. 3.37
☐ C. 3.47
☐ D. 3.57

27) A juice container holds 1.2 liters. An identical container holds 1,200 milliliters. Which container holds more juice?

☐ A. The first (1.2 L) holds more
☐ B. The second (1,200 mL) holds more
☐ C. They hold the same amount
☐ D. Cannot determine from the information

28) Write 10^4 as a standard number.

Record your answer in the space provided.

29) A classroom model measures 8 feet long, 5 feet wide, and 5 feet tall. What is its volume?

☐ A. 40 cubic feet
☐ B. 25 cubic feet
☐ C. 200 cubic feet
☐ D. 18 cubic feet

30) A model shows 3 wholes divided into sixths. Which equation finds the number of sixths?

☐ A. $\frac{1}{6} \div 3 = n$
☐ B. $3 + \frac{1}{6} = n$
☐ C. $3 \times \frac{1}{6} = n$
☐ D. $3 \div \frac{1}{6} = n$

31) Subtract: $7\frac{2}{10} - 3\frac{7}{10}$.

☐ A. $3\frac{1}{10}$
☐ B. $4\frac{5}{10}$
☐ C. $4\frac{1}{2}$
☐ D. $3\frac{1}{2}$

32) A comparison shows four scaled bars for four expressions. Which expression has the greatest value?

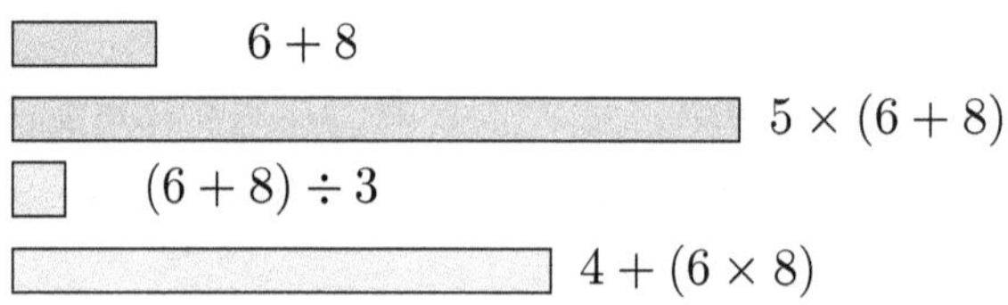

☐ A. $6 + 8$
☐ B. $5 \times (6 + 8)$
☐ C. $(6 + 8) \div 3$
☐ D. $4 + (6 \times 8)$

33)

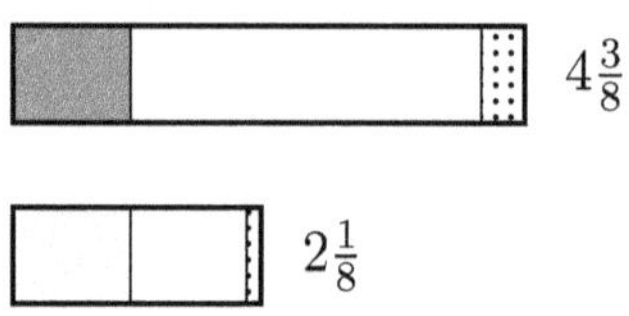

Add: $4\frac{3}{8} + 2\frac{1}{8}$

☐ A. $6\frac{1}{4}$
☐ B. $6\frac{1}{2}$
☐ C. $6\frac{3}{8}$
☐ D. 7

34) Pattern X is $1, 2, 3, 4$. Pattern Y is $4, 8, 12, 16$. Each Y value is how many times X?

Record your answer in the space provided.

35) Divide: $567 \div 21$

☐ A. 25
☐ B. 31
☐ C. 29
☐ D. 27

36) A table shows products when multiplying 3.6 by different numbers. Complete the pattern.

Multiply 3.6 by:	Product
0.5	1.8
1	3.6
2	7.2
4	?

☐ A. 10.8
☐ B. 12.4
☐ C. 14.4
☐ D. 15.2

37) A recipe uses $1\frac{1}{2}$ cups of milk and $\frac{1}{2}$ cup of water. How many fluid ounces of liquid is that in all?
Use: 1 cup = 8 fl oz

Milk $1\frac{1}{2}$ cups	+	Water $\frac{1}{2}$ cup

Total cups → fluid ounces

☐ A. 8 fl oz
☐ B. 12 fl oz
☐ C. 16 fl oz
☐ D. 20 fl oz

38) What is 5.678 rounded to the nearest hundredth?

☐ A. 5.67
☐ B. 5.68
☐ C. 5.7
☐ D. 6.0

39) Pattern A is $1, 2, 3, 4, \ldots$ and Pattern B is $3, 6, 9, 12, \ldots$. If Pattern A gives the x-value and Pattern B gives the y-value, what ordered pair comes next?

☐ A. $(4, 15)$
☐ B. $(5, 12)$
☐ C. $(6, 15)$
☐ D. $(5, 15)$

40) Number line: Start at $\frac{9}{10}$. Back by $\frac{3}{10}$.

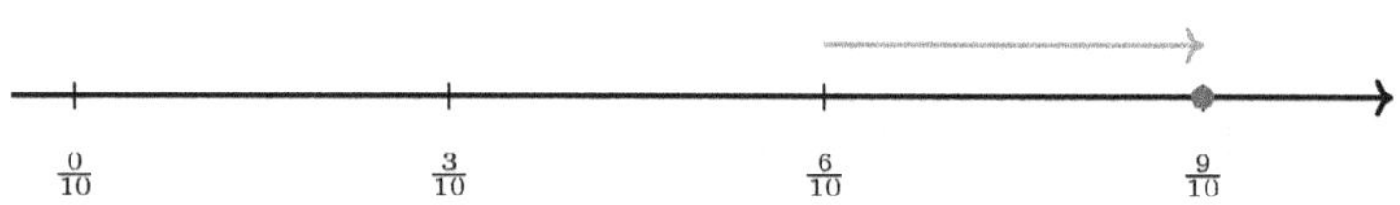

Where do you land?

☐ A. $\frac{5}{10}$
☐ B. $\frac{6}{10}$
☐ C. $\frac{7}{10}$
☐ D. $\frac{8}{10}$

End of Practice Test

Take a short breath, then check your work with care. Good corrections can teach almost as much as the test itself.

Time Traveler Triumph!

You've Journeyed Through All 8 Practice Tests!

You're a Math Time Traveler!

Time-jump complete! You traveled through all 8 practice tests—that's 320 math problems. With each leap, you added new skills to your math toolkit and grew braver under pressure.

Your Time-Traveling Triumphs:

- Time-traveled through 8 full practice tests (320 questions!)
- Built stamina for a full 40-question test
- Practiced strategy and steady checking
- Learned from past mistakes and re-wrote them as wins
- Built confidence that lasts through any era

Your timeline looks bright! On test day, you'll bring everything you've practiced.

Your Time-Travel Log!

Mark Each Stop on Your Timeline

Record the date and score for each leap:

Test	Date	Score	Notes
Test 1		/40	
Test 2		/40	
Test 3		/40	
Test 4		/40	
Test 5		/40	
Test 6		/40	
Test 7		/40	
Test 8		/40	

Time Traveler's Thoughts:

- Which test felt like the wildest leap?
- Which strategy from the past helped you the most?
- What would you tell yourself before Test 1?
- How will you use these skills in the future?

Test-day tip: Read carefully, show your work, and check that your answer makes sense.

Your math journey across time is just beginning. Keep leaping!

Practice Test Answer Keys

How to use this section:

1. check your answer
2. circle missed questions
3. rework them before reading the explanation

Good correction habits build strong scores.

Answer Key for Practice Test 1

#	Answer	#	Answer
1	A	26	D
2	C	27	A
3	B	28	A
4	B	29	D
5	A	30	C
6	A	31	A
7	C	32	B
8	C	33	C
9	A	34	A
10	6 ft	35	C
11	B	36	B
12	C	37	A
13	D	38	A
14	D	39	20 mi
15	A	40	A
16	B		
17	D		
18	A, B		
19	A		
20	D		
21	D		
22	1		
23	C		
24	$\frac{12}{16}$		
25	$\frac{1}{8}$		

Answer Key for Practice Test 2

#	Answer	#	Answer
1	B	26	C
2	C	27	B
3	C	28	D
4	A	29	D
5	D	30	A
6	D	31	B
7	A	32	D
8	$5 \div \frac{1}{4} = n$	33	D
9	A	34	B
10	3	35	D
11	A	36	B
12	C	37	B
13	$4\frac{1}{2}$ L	38	C
14	6	39	$4\frac{1}{4}$
15	A	40	D
16	D		
17	D		
18	C		
19	C		
20	A		
21	A, B		
22	C		
23	C		
24	D		
25	B		

Answer Key for Practice Test 3

#	Answer	#	Answer
1	D	26	D
2	D	27	$<$
3	about 8	28	D
4	D	29	A
5	C	30	D
6	B	31	C
7	C	32	$2\frac{3}{4}$
8	D	33	B
9	B	34	B
10	B	35	C
11	D	36	C
12	D	37	D
13	B	38	B
14	C	39	D
15	A	40	A
16	C		
17	D		
18	A		
19	C		
20	A, B		
21	42		
22	A		
23	A		
24	42		
25	D		

Answer Key for Practice Test 4

#	Answer	#	Answer
1	C	26	D
2	D	27	A
3	A	28	B
4	D	29	720000
5	D	30	A
6	$3\frac{1}{2}$	31	A
7	D	32	B
8	C	33	C
9	D	34	A
10	A	35	24
11	B	36	A
12	C	37	A
13	B	38	B
14	48	39	A
15	C	40	B
16	D		
17	D		
18	D		
19	A, B		
20	A		
21	D		
22	500 m^3		
23	D		
24	B		
25	A		

Answer Key for Practice Test 5

Q	Answer	Q	Answer
1	D	26	C
2	D	27	C
3	B	28	C
4	B	29	A
5	A	30	$(4, 20)$
6	B	31	3645
7	B	32	D
8	A	33	B
9	0.45	34	B
10	A	35	D
11	C	36	D
12	A	37	A
13	B	38	$\frac{3}{8}$
14	B	39	B
15	$\frac{5}{9}$	40	D
16	B		
17	D		
18	C		
19	B		
20	B		
21	C		
22	B, C, D		
23	A		
24	C		
25	B		

Answer Key for Practice Test 6

Q	Answer	Q	Answer
1	C	26	C
2	B	27	A
3	B	28	C
4	B	29	132 cm^3
5	D	30	D
6	$\frac{3}{5}$	31	D
7	D	32	D
8	A	33	B
9	A	34	D
10	B	35	D
11	C	36	A
12	B	37	A
13	A	38	2
14	$\frac{7}{12}$	39	72 cubic feet
15	D	40	D
16	B		
17	C		
18	A, B		
19	B		
20	A		
21	C		
22	A		
23	D		
24	B		
25	D		

Answer Key for Practice Test 7

#	Answer	#	Answer
1	B	26	B
2	12	27	B
3	A	28	B
4	B	29	A
5	B	30	D
6	A	31	C
7	7.5 m	32	3 sides
8	D	33	C
9	D	34	70
10	B	35	A
11	D	36	B
12	D	37	D
13	C	38	A
14	D	39	D
15	$3\frac{5}{8}$	40	C
16	D		
17	A		
18	A, C		
19	C		
20	D		
21	D		
22	D		
23	C		
24	B		
25	D		

Answer Key for Practice Test 8

#	Answer	#	Answer
1	B	26	A
2	D	27	C
3	6	28	10000
4	B	29	C
5	C	30	D
6	A	31	D
7	0.067	32	B
8	C	33	B
9	C	34	4
10	B	35	D
11	C	36	C
12	D	37	C
13	C	38	B
14	C	39	D
15	C	40	B
16	C		
17	B		
18	B		
19	A, B		
20	B		
21	40		
22	B		
23	D		
24	B		
25	B		

Practice Test Answers and Explanations

Practice Test 1 Answers and Explanations

1) **Choice A is correct.** [MA.5.GR.1.1] A pentagon is a polygon with 5 straight sides and 5 vertices. A quadrilateral has 4 sides, and a rectangle is a type of quadrilateral.
2) **Choice C is correct.** [MA.5.FR.2.3] A, B, D are all true. C is FALSE: $8.4 \div 10 = 0.84$, not 8.4. (Dividing doesn't leave the number unchanged.)
3) **Choice B is correct.** [MA.5.FR.2.1] LCM(5,4) = 20. $\frac{3}{5} = \frac{12}{20}$ and $\frac{1}{4} = \frac{5}{20}$. $\frac{12}{20} + \frac{5}{20} = \frac{17}{20}$ meter.
4) **Choice B is correct.** [MA.5.GR.1.2] A rhombus is a quadrilateral with all sides equal. If opposite angles are also equal, it is a rhombus (not necessarily a square).
5) **Choice A is correct.** [MA.5.GR.4.1] The student confused the order. The correct pair is $(3, 5)$: 3 units right (x-coordinate) and 5 units up (y-coordinate). The student wrote $(5, 3)$, which swaps them.
6) **Choice A is correct.** [MA.5.FR.2.1] $\frac{1}{2}$ and $\frac{2}{3}$ have different denominators. With LCD 6: $\frac{1}{2} = \frac{3}{6} \neq \frac{4}{6} = \frac{2}{3}$.
7) **Choice C is correct.** [MA.5.AR.1.1] Multiply: $18.50 \times 20 = 370$ dollars per week.
8) **Choice C is correct.** [MA.5.AR.1.1] The base is $14 \times 10 = 140$ square feet. With a height of 8 feet, the volume is $140 \times 8 = 1{,}120$ cubic feet.
9) **Choice A is correct.** [MA.5.AR.2.2] Evaluate each option to be sure. A gives $25 \times 4 = 100$, while B gives 180, C gives 29, and D gives 105. Only A is exactly 100.
10) **The correct answer is 6 ft.** [MA.5.GR.3.1] The base area is $7 \times 5 = 35$ square feet. Since $210 \div 35 = 6$, the height is 6 ft.
11) **Choice B is correct.** [MA.5.GR.3.1] $105 \times 10 = 1050$. Append one zero to 105.
12) **Choice C is correct.** [MA.5.FR.2.3] Add: $2\frac{1}{3} + 3\frac{2}{3} = 5\frac{3}{3} = 6$ ft.
13) **Choice D is correct.** [MA.5.GR.2.1] In an area model, divide one dimension into 2 equal parts (for $\frac{1}{2}$) and the other into 3 equal parts (for $\frac{1}{3}$). The overlapping shaded region is 1 out of 6 total squares, so the product is $\frac{1}{6}$.
14) **Choice D is correct.** [MA.5.AR.2.1] The tape diagram shows A as one unit. B is made of two of those same units, so B is twice A.
15) **Choice A is correct.** [MA.5.GR.4.2] Adding the same input twice is the same as multiplying it by 2. So $x + x$ can be written as $2x$.
16) **Choice B is correct.** [MA.5.NSO.2.2] $735 \div 15 = 49$. Check: $15 \times 49 = 735$.
17) **Choice D is correct.** [MA.5.NSO.2.2] 1 gallon = 4 quarts = 8 pints = 16 cups. So 3 gallons = $3 \times 16 = 48$ cups.
18) **Choices A, B are correct.** [MA.5.GR.1.1] Every triangle has exactly 3 sides and 3 vertices. Some triangles have a right angle, but many triangles do not.
19) **Choice A is correct.** [MA.5.GR.4.2] Dividing each term in Sequence 1 by 5 gives Sequence 2: $5 \div 5 = 1$, $10 \div 5 = 2$, $15 \div 5 = 3$, etc.
20) **Choice D is correct.** [MA.5.GR.3.3] Use the rectangular-prism volume formula: $12 \times 7 \times 2 = 168$. So the volume is 168 cubic meters.
21) **Choice D is correct.** [MA.5.FR.2.3] $1\frac{3}{4} \times 8 = \frac{7}{4} \times 8 = \frac{56}{4} = 14$ yards.
22) **The correct answer is 1.** [MA.5.AR.1.2] $\frac{2}{3} \times \frac{3}{2} = 1$ liter.
23) **Choice C is correct.** [MA.5.AR.1.2] Division comes first: $18 \div 6 = 3$. Now the expression is $3 + 3 - 1$, which equals 5.
24) **The correct answer is $\frac{12}{16}$.** [MA.5.AR.2.2] Multiply numerator and denominator by 4: $\frac{3\times4}{4\times4} = \frac{12}{16}$.
25) **The correct answer is $\frac{1}{8}$.** [MA.5.FR.2.1] $\frac{1}{4} \div 2 = \frac{1}{4} \times \frac{1}{2} = \frac{1}{8}$.
26) **Choice D is correct.** [MA.5.AR.1.3] A power of 10 tells how many factors of 10 to use. $10^6 = 1000000$ has 6 zeros. This confirms the answer.
27) **Choice A is correct.** [MA.5.AR.1.2] Shipped: $\frac{1}{4} + \frac{1}{3} = \frac{3}{12} + \frac{4}{12} = \frac{7}{12}$. Remaining: $1 - \frac{7}{12} = \frac{5}{12}$.
28) **Choice A is correct.** [MA.5.NSO.1.3] 0.6 (6 tenths) $>$ 0.06 (6 hundredths). A rise of 0.6 degrees is 10 times larger.
29) **Choice D is correct.** [MA.5.FR.2.3] $0.5 \div 10{,}000$ moves the decimal four places left, giving 0.00005.
30) **Choice C is correct.** [MA.5.FR.2.3] LCD = 20. $\frac{7}{10} = \frac{14}{20}$; $\frac{1}{4} = \frac{5}{20}$. $\frac{14}{20} - \frac{5}{20} = \frac{9}{20}$.

31) **Choice A is correct.** (MA.5.FR.2.2) $\frac{7}{15} \approx 0.47$ and $\frac{5}{13} \approx 0.38$, so true sum ≈ 0.85. Estimate is 1. Difference: $1 - 0.85 = 0.15 < 0.5$. The estimate is reasonable.

32) **Choice B is correct.** (MA.5.NSO.1.1) The number 12.345 breaks down as: 12 (ones and tens), 0.3 (tenths), 0.04 (hundredths), 0.005 (thousandths).

33) **Choice C is correct.** (MA.5.NSO.2.4) When the tenths digit is exactly 5, we round up. So 4.5 rounds to 5.

34) **Choice A is correct.** (MA.5.NSO.2.4) First translate "the product of 3 and 5" as 3×5. The difference of 25 and that product is $25 - 3 \times 5$.

35) **Choice C is correct.** (MA.5.FR.2.3) Multiply $5 \times 0.75 = 3.75$. Since 0.75 has 2 decimal places and 5 has 0, the product has 2 decimal places: \$3.75.

36) **Choice B is correct.** (MA.5.NSO.2.2) Add the four partial products: $(20 \times 10) + (5 \times 10) + (20 \times 3) + (5 \times 3) = 200 + 50 + 60 + 15 = 325$.

37) **Choice A is correct.** (MA.5.GR.1.2) A geometric circle has a curved boundary, so it is not a polygon, a quadrilateral, or a rectangle.

38) **Choice A is correct.** (MA.5.GR.4.2) Rule A: 1, 4, 7, 10. Rule B: 0, 4, 8, 12. Pairs (Rule A, Rule B) are listed in choice A.

39) **The correct answer is 20 mi.** (MA.5.GR.4.2) The x-coordinate is 4, so it shows 4 hours. The y-coordinate is 20, so it shows 20 miles. Accept equivalent interpretations that correctly match 4 with hours and 20 with miles.

40) **Choice A is correct.** (MA.5.FR.2.1) Use sixths: $8\frac{1}{3} = 8\frac{2}{6}$. Regroup as $7\frac{8}{6}$. Then $7\frac{8}{6} - 2\frac{5}{6} = 5\frac{3}{6} = 5\frac{1}{2}$.

Practice Test 2 Answers and Explanations

1) **Choice B is correct.** (MA.5.NSO.1.1) In 9.452, the digit 5 is in the hundredths place, so it is worth 0.05. The digit 2 is in the thousandths place, so it is worth 0.002.

2) **Choice C is correct.** (MA.5.GR.4.1) The differences are 3, 5, 7, and 9. The next difference is 11, so $27 + 11 = 38$.

3) **Choice C is correct.** (MA.5.GR.4.1) Dividing by 1,000 moves the decimal point three places to the left. $8,000 \div 1,000 = 8$.

4) **Choice A is correct.** (MA.5.FR.2.3) The basic fact is $3 \times 4 = 12$. The factors 300 and 400 have four zeros total, making 120,000, which has 4 trailing zeros.

5) **Choice D is correct.** (MA.5.AR.1.3) $9 \div \frac{1}{4} = 9 \times 4 = 36$. There are 36 bundles.

6) **Choice D is correct.** (MA.5.GR.3.3) The known length and height make groups of $15 \times 9 = 135$ cubic centimeters. Since $540 \div 135 = 4$, the width is 4 cm.

7) **Choice A is correct.** (MA.5.M.2.1) Total: $18.5 + 21.75 + 19.25 + 18 = 77.5$ kg. Remaining: $80 - 77.5 = 2.5$ kg.

8) **The correct answer is $5 \div \frac{1}{4} = n$.** (MA.5.AR.1.3) The total is 5 cups and each serving is one fourth cup, so divide total by serving size.

9) **Choice A is correct.** (MA.5.AR.1.3) All four sides are equal: $5 - 1 = 4$ units. All four angles are right angles. This is a square.

10) **The correct answer is 3.** (MA.5.FR.2.3) First simplify $\frac{2}{6}$ to $\frac{1}{3}$. Then $9 \times \frac{1}{3} = \frac{9}{3} = 3$.

11) **Choice A is correct.** (MA.5.FR.2.3) Convert all to meters: 5,000 mm = 5 m, 50 m = 50 m, 0.5 km = 500 m, and 600 cm = 6 m. The smallest is 5,000 mm, which is 5 m.

12) **Choice C is correct.** (MA.5.M.1.1) A rectangular prism is a 3D solid figure, so it has volume. A line segment, rectangle, and point are not solid figures with interior space.

13) **The correct answer is $4\frac{1}{2}$ L.** (MA.5.DP.1.1) Add the measurements shown: $\frac{1}{2} + \frac{3}{4} + \frac{3}{4} + 1 + 1\frac{1}{2} = 4\frac{1}{2}$ liters.

14) **The correct answer is 6.** (MA.5.NSO.1.2) In 4.06, the 6 is in the hundredths place.

15) **Choice A is correct.** (MA.5.NSO.1.2) The first expression makes 3 copies of $20 - 5$. The second expression subtracts 3 copies of 5 from only one 20. The first expression is greater.

16) **Choice D is correct.** (MA.5.FR.2.3) $\frac{2}{3} < 1$, so $7 \times \frac{2}{3} < 7 \times 1$.

17) **Choice D is correct.** (MA.5.FR.2.1) LCD of 3 and 5 is 15. $\frac{1}{3} = \frac{5}{15}$ and $\frac{2}{5} = \frac{6}{15}$.

18) **Choice C is correct.** (MA.5.FR.2.1) Picture A shows $\frac{2}{3}$ (two thirds). Picture B shows $\frac{4}{6}$ (four sixths). Since $\frac{2}{3} = \frac{4}{6}$, both pictures represent the same amount.

19) **Choice C is correct.** (MA.5.AR.1.1) Books cost: $3 \times 12.95 = 38.85$ dollars. Pens cost: $5 \times 2.50 = 12.50$ dollars. Total: $38.85 + 12.50 = 51.35$ dollars.

20) **Choice A is correct.** (MA.5.GR.4.2) The x-coordinate is the time in hours, 9, and the y-coordinate is the temperature, 15 degrees Celsius.
21) **Choices A, B are correct.** (MA.5.AR.1.3) Each whole has 5 fifths, so 4 wholes have $4 \times 5 = 20$ fifths. Choices C and D use a common miscount of 4 groups of 4 instead of 4 groups of 5.
22) **Choice C is correct.** (MA.5.GR.3.2) Find each part first: Prism A is $8 \times 2 \times 3 = 48$ cubic feet, and Prism B is $3 \times 5 \times 5 = 75$ cubic feet. Because the parts do not overlap, add them: $48 + 75 = 123$ cubic feet.
23) **Choice C is correct.** (MA.5.GR.3.1) Multiply the three dimensions: $9 \times 4 \times 3 = 36 \times 3 = 108$. The volume is 108 cm^3.
24) **Choice D is correct.** (MA.5.FR.2.3) To convert meters to centimeters, multiply by 100: $1.5 \times 100 = 150$ cm.
25) **Choice B is correct.** (MA.5.FR.2.3) When multiplying by 10, each digit shifts one place left: 4 (tens) →4 (hundreds), 2 (ones) →2 (tens), 0 fills the ones place.
26) **Choice C is correct.** (MA.5.AR.2.2) First solve the parentheses: $7 + 3 = 10$. Then multiply, $6 \times 10 = 60$, and subtract 20 to get 40.
27) **Choice B is correct.** (MA.5.AR.2.2) B is correct because $4.26 + 1.53 = 5.79$. A should be 5.49, C should be 8.43, and D should be 8.65.
28) **Choice D is correct.** (MA.5.GR.1.2) The hierarchy shows that Square is a child of Rectangle, meaning every square is also a rectangle. Not every rectangle is a square.
29) **Choice D is correct.** (MA.5.AR.1.3) The repeated part is $\frac{1}{4}$ mile. $5 \div \frac{1}{4} = 5 \times 4 = 20$, so she can plan 20 repeats.
30) **Choice A is correct.** (MA.5.AR.1.2) $\frac{3}{4} \times \frac{1}{4} = \frac{3}{16}$ km.
31) **Choice B is correct.** (MA.5.FR.2.3) $36 \times \frac{2}{9} = \frac{72}{9} = 8$ crayons. The fraction is less than 1, so the product is smaller than the original amount.
32) **Choice D is correct.** (MA.5.AR.1.3) $\frac{1}{8} \div 3 = \frac{1}{8} \times \frac{1}{3} = \frac{1}{24}$.
33) **Choice D is correct.** (MA.5.FR.2.3) Check each: A is $\frac{1}{6}$ not $\frac{1}{5}$. B is $\frac{4}{9}$ not $\frac{4}{6}$. C is $\frac{3}{16}$ not $\frac{4}{16}$. D is correct.
34) **Choice B is correct.** (MA.5.GR.1.1) Two equal sides (10 m each) make it isosceles. In isosceles triangles, the two angles opposite the equal sides are also equal.
35) **Choice D is correct.** (MA.5.GR.3.1) The base has $3 \times 5 = 15$ cubes. Since $60 \div 15 = 4$, the prism has 4 layers, so the height is 4 units.
36) **Choice B is correct.** (MA.5.GR.3.1) The room is exactly filled, so compare volumes. Room volume: $18 \times 12 \times 10 = 2160$ cubic feet. Number of boxes: $2160 \div 360 = 6$ boxes.
37) **Choice B is correct.** (MA.5.GR.4.1) The y-coordinate is 6. Half of 6 is 3, so the x-coordinate is 3. The ordered pair is $(3, 6)$.
38) **Choice C is correct.** (MA.5.NSO.2.3) Line up decimal points and subtract place by place. Unknown subtrahend: $15.42 - 8.67 = 6.75$. This confirms the answer.
39) **The correct answer is $4\frac{1}{4}$.** (MA.5.DP.1.1) Count the X marks above each length. The length $4\frac{1}{4}$ has 3 X marks, more than any other pencil length.
40) **Choice D is correct.** (MA.5.GR.3.1) The known width and height make groups of $5 \times 4 = 20$ cubic units. Since $120 \div 20 = 6$, the length is 6 units.

Practice Test 3 Answers and Explanations

1) **Choice D is correct.** (MA.5.GR.1.2) Every rectangle has two pairs of parallel sides, so every rectangle is a parallelogram.
2) **Choice D is correct.** (MA.5.NSO.1.2) "Two and thirty-seven hundredths" means 2 whole units and 37 hundredths: 2.37.
3) **The correct answer is about 8.** (MA.5.NSO.1.2) $5\frac{1}{6} \approx 5$ and $2\frac{7}{8} \approx 3$, so the sum is about 8. Accept equivalent estimates that are clearly close to 8.
4) **Choice D is correct.** (MA.5.FR.2.2) A, B, C all equal 0.73. D: $73 \div 10 = 7.3$ (not equal to 0.73).
5) **Choice C is correct.** (MA.5.FR.2.3) The strip starts with one eighth, then shares that small amount into 3 parts. So the matching division equation is $\frac{1}{8} \div 3 = ?$.
6) **Choice B is correct.** (MA.5.AR.1.3) Use total amount divided by the size of one piece. The equation is $2 \div \frac{1}{5} = n$.
7) **Choice C is correct.** (MA.5.DP.1.1) Highest score is 6, lowest is 2. Difference: $6 - 2 = 4$.
8) **Choice D is correct.** (MA.5.DP.1.1) The pieces longer than 1 inch are two pieces of $1\frac{1}{4}$ inches and one piece of $1\frac{1}{2}$ inches. Their total is $1\frac{1}{4} + 1\frac{1}{4} + 1\frac{1}{2} = 4$ inches.

9) **Choice B is correct.** (MA.5.FR.2.3) There are 5 groups of $\frac{2}{7}$, so multiply 5×2 in the numerator: $5 \times \frac{2}{7} = \frac{10}{7} = 1\frac{3}{7}$.

10) **Choice B is correct.** (MA.5.FR.2.1) LCM(3,4) = 12. $\frac{2}{3} = \frac{8}{12}$ and $\frac{3}{4} = \frac{9}{12}$. $\frac{8}{12} + \frac{9}{12} = \frac{17}{12} = 1\frac{5}{12}$.

11) **Choice D is correct.** (MA.5.AR.2.1) The expression $(18 \times 5) + 3$ is the value of 18×5 with 3 added. So it is 3 more than 18×5.

12) **Choice D is correct.** (MA.5.M.1.1) Since 12 inches = 1 foot, divide 54 by 12: $54 \div 12 = 4\frac{6}{12} = 4\frac{1}{2}$ feet.

13) **Choice B is correct.** (MA.5.FR.2.1) $\frac{1}{5} = \frac{2}{10}$. $\frac{8}{10} - \frac{2}{10} = \frac{6}{10} = \frac{3}{5}$.

14) **Choice C is correct.** (MA.5.FR.2.1) $1\frac{1}{2} \times 1\frac{1}{2} = \frac{3}{2} \times \frac{3}{2} = \frac{9}{4} = 2\frac{1}{4}$ square inches.

15) **Choice A is correct.** (MA.5.NSO.2.2) Use compatible numbers: $2,345 \approx 2,400$ and $59 \approx 60$. So $2,400 \div 60 = 40$.

16) **Choice C is correct.** (MA.5.FR.2.3) 300 has two zeros and 20 has one zero. Since $3 \times 2 = 6$, the product is 6,000.

17) **Choice D is correct.** (MA.5.FR.2.3) The number line shows 1.2 divided into four jumps of 0.3 each. Therefore, $1.2 \div 0.3 = 4$.

18) **Choice A is correct.** (MA.5.GR.4.2) Index 1: 2. Index 2: $2 + 3 = 5$. Index 3: $5 + 3 = 8$. Index 4: $8 + 3 = 11$.

19) **Choice C is correct.** (MA.5.M.1.1) Convert all to mL: A = 800 mL, B = 850 mL, C = 750 mL. Since $750 < 800 < 850$, Sample C is smallest.

20) **Choices A, B are correct.** (MA.5.GR.4.2) For $(4, 3)$, the first number tells you to move 4 right, and the second number tells you to move 3 up. Choices C and D switch those two moves.

21) **The correct answer is 42.** (MA.5.AR.2.2) Do the multiplications first: $8 \times 6 = 48$ and $2 \times 5 = 10$. Then subtract left to right: $100 - 48 - 10 = 42$.

22) **Choice A is correct.** (MA.5.AR.2.2) The gift and card together cost $42 + 3$ dollars. Since 6 friends share that total, divide the whole sum by 6.

23) **Choice A is correct.** (MA.5.FR.2.1) Common denominator is 8: $13\frac{6}{8} - 6\frac{5}{8} = 7\frac{1}{8}$ ft.

24) **The correct answer is 42.** (MA.5.AR.1.3) Each whole contains 6 sixths. Seven wholes contain $7 \times 6 = 42$ sixths, so the quotient is 42.

25) **Choice D is correct.** (MA.5.AR.1.3) Use the rectangular-prism volume formula: $6 \times 7 \times 7 = 294$. So the volume is 294 cubic meters.

26) **Choice D is correct.** (MA.5.GR.3.1) A cube that is 1 meter on each edge is 100 centimeters on each edge. It would have 100 layers, with $100 \times 100 = 10,000$ cubic centimeters in each layer. So $10,000 \times 100 = 1,000,000$ cubic centimeters.

27) **The correct answer is $<$.** (MA.5.NSO.1.3) Tenths are equal (both 3). Hundredths: 4 vs. 8; since $4 < 8$, $0.342 < 0.386$.

28) **Choice D is correct.** (MA.5.NSO.1.3) Add the grams first: $25 + 50 + 225 = 300$ grams. Since 1,000 grams make 1 kilogram, $300 \div 1,000 = 0.3$ kilograms.

29) **Choice A is correct.** (MA.5.GR.2.1) The blue region is 2 out of 5. The red region is 3 out of 4. The double-shaded overlap has 6 squares out of a total of 20, so the product is $\frac{6}{20}$.

30) **Choice D is correct.** (MA.5.FR.2.3) Dividing by 1,000 moves the decimal three places left, so 8.1 becomes 0.0081.

31) **Choice C is correct.** (MA.5.FR.2.3) $10^5 = 100000$ and $10^6 = 1000000$, so this is true.

32) **The correct answer is $2\frac{3}{4}$.** (MA.5.FR.2.3) $4\frac{1}{2} = 4\frac{2}{4} = 3\frac{6}{4}$. Subtract: $3\frac{6}{4} - 1\frac{3}{4} = 2\frac{3}{4}$.

33) **Choice B is correct.** (MA.5.AR.1.2) Convert to fourths: $2\frac{1}{2} = 2\frac{2}{4}$. Add: $1\frac{3}{4} + 2\frac{2}{4} = 3\frac{5}{4} = 4\frac{1}{4}$.

34) **Choice B is correct.** (MA.5.FR.2.3) $5,200 \div 100 = 52$. Marcus only divided by 10; Kevin divided by 1,000; Aisha did not divide.

35) **Choice C is correct.** (MA.5.NSO.2.4) Compare distances from 0.5: 0.45 is 0.05 away, 0.489 is 0.011 away, 0.501 is 0.001 away, and 0.55 is 0.05 away. The closest number is 0.501.

36) **Choice C is correct.** (MA.5.NSO.2.2) $21 \times 13 = (20 + 1) \times 13 = (20 \times 13) + (1 \times 13) = 260 + 13 = 273$ (Riley). Also, $21 \times 13 = 21 \times (10 + 3) = (21 \times 10) + (21 \times 3) = 210 + 63 = 273$ (Jamal). Piper made an error; the correct answer is 273, not 260.

37) **Choice D is correct.** (MA.5.GR.4.2) For $x = 1$: $4(1) = 4$ check; for $x = 2$: $4(2) = 8$ check; for $x = 3$: $4(3) = 12$ check.

38) **Choice B is correct.** (MA.5.GR.4.1) The first pattern adds 8 each time. The second pattern multiplies by 2 each time, so it follows a different rule.

39) **Choice D is correct.** (MA.5.GR.1.1) The right trapezoid shown has 2 right angles (on the left side, marked with squares) and 2 non-right angles on the right.

40) **Choice A is correct.** (MA.5.GR.3.3) Check the student's height: $8 \times 5 \times 6 = 240$, not 160. The base area is $8 \times 5 = 40$ square centimeters, and $160 \div 40 = 4$, so the correct height is 4 cm.

Practice Test 4 Answers and Explanations

1) **Choice C is correct.** (MA.5.GR.3.1) Volume measures the amount of space inside a solid figure, so it is measured in cubic units such as cubic inches.
2) **Choice D is correct.** (MA.5.AR.2.1) Choice D has the smaller first factor and the smaller second factor. So 7×7 must be the smallest product.
3) **Choice A is correct.** (MA.5.GR.3.2) The first prism is $6 \times 4 \times 4 = 96$ cubic meters. The second is $6 \times 4 \times 3 = 72$ cubic meters. Together they make 168 cubic meters.
4) **Choice D is correct.** (MA.5.GR.1.1) An obtuse triangle has one angle greater than 90 degrees. Since 120 degrees is greater than 90 degrees, this is an obtuse triangle.
5) **Choice D is correct.** (MA.5.AR.2.2) The tree says to find each branch first: $8 + 2 = 10$ and $7 - 3 = 4$. Then multiply the two results: $10 \times 4 = 40$.
6) **The correct answer is $3\frac{1}{2}$.** (MA.5.FR.2.3) Convert both mixed numbers first: $1\frac{1}{2} = \frac{3}{2}$ and $2\frac{1}{3} = \frac{7}{3}$. Then $\frac{3}{2} \times \frac{7}{3} = \frac{21}{6} = \frac{7}{2} = 3\frac{1}{2}$.
7) **Choice D is correct.** (MA.5.FR.2.3) $\frac{7}{10} = 0.7$ (tenths) and $\frac{1}{100} = 0.01$ (hundredths), so $4 + 0.7 + 0.01 = 4.71$.
8) **Choice C is correct.** (MA.5.NSO.1.2) $\frac{3}{2} > 1$, so the product is greater than 18.
9) **Choice D is correct.** (MA.5.AR.1.1) Add the donations: $284.75 + 156.50 + 320.25 = 761.50$. Then subtract the cost of the books: $761.50 - 450.00 = 311.50$.
10) **Choice A is correct.** (MA.5.GR.4.2) The plotted point is at 6 on the time axis and 150 on the distance axis. It represents 6 hours and 150 miles.
11) **Choice B is correct.** (MA.5.FR.2.1) Grid A: $\frac{20}{100} = \frac{1}{5}$. Grid B: $\frac{40}{100} = \frac{2}{5}$.
12) **Choice C is correct.** (MA.5.AR.1.2) Convert: $\frac{3}{4} = \frac{6}{8}$. Then $\frac{6}{8} + \frac{2}{8} = \frac{8}{8} = 1$ mile total.
13) **Choice B is correct.** (MA.5.NSO.1.3) Compare tenths first, then hundredths when needed: $0.72 < 0.80 < 0.86 < 1.0$.
14) **The correct answer is 48.** (MA.5.FR.2.3) Move the decimal point one place left: $480 \to 48$.
15) **Choice C is correct.** (MA.5.FR.2.3) Add the amounts shown: $\frac{1}{4} + 2(\frac{1}{2}) + 2(\frac{3}{4}) + 1 + 1\frac{1}{4} = 5$ cups.
16) **Choice D is correct.** (MA.5.FR.2.3) Multiply by 1000 (1 thousand): $1.25 \times 1000 = 1250$ people.
17) **Choice D is correct.** (MA.5.FR.2.3) The base has $7 \times 4 = 28$ unit cubes. Since $56 \div 28 = 2$, the prism is 2 units tall.
18) **Choice D is correct.** (MA.5.DP.1.1) Count X marks at 2, $2\frac{1}{2}$, and 3 inches: $4 + 2 + 1 = 7$ measurements.
19) **Choices A, B are correct.** (MA.5.GR.4.2) C reverses growth; D is false ($15 \neq 30$).
20) **Choice A is correct.** (MA.5.NSO.2.3) Hundredths: $75 + 38 = 113$ hundredths, which is 1 whole and 13 hundredths. Add that extra whole to $1 + 2$: the correct sum is 4.13. Nice careful regrouping keeps each place value in its place.
21) **Choice D is correct.** (MA.5.GR.1.2) The opposite sides are parallel, so the figure is a parallelogram. Since no angles are right angles, it is not a rectangle.
22) **The correct answer is 500 m^3.** (MA.5.GR.3.1) $25 \times 10 \times 2 = 500\ m^3$.
23) **Choice D is correct.** (MA.5.GR.3.1) Use total amount divided by the size of one piece. The equation is $10 \div \frac{1}{5} = n$.
24) **Choice B is correct.** (MA.5.FR.2.2) $1\frac{1}{12} \approx 1$ and $\frac{7}{8} \approx 1$. So $1\frac{1}{12} + \frac{7}{8} \approx 1 + 1 = 2$. All others sum to less than 1.
25) **Choice A is correct.** (MA.5.AR.1.3) $6 \div \frac{1}{2} = 6 \times 2 = 12$.
26) **Choice D is correct.** (MA.5.AR.1.3) The table shows $25.4 \div 10 = 2.54$. Decimal moves 1 place left.
27) **Choice A is correct.** (MA.5.GR.4.2) All four sides are equal: each side is $8 - 2 = 6$ units long. All angles are right angles. This is a square.
28) **Choice B is correct.** (MA.5.GR.3.1) Volume $= 10 \times 8 \times 4 = 80 \times 4 = 320\ in^3$.
29) **The correct answer is 720000.** (MA.5.FR.2.3) Use $8 \times 9 = 72$. The factors 80 and 9,000 have four zeros total, so the product is 720,000.
30) **Choice A is correct.** (MA.5.FR.2.3) She waters $\frac{1}{4}$ of the $\frac{7}{12}$ corn section, so multiply: $\frac{1}{4} \times \frac{7}{12} = \frac{7}{48}$ of the whole field.
31) **Choice A is correct.** (MA.5.FR.2.3) $8 \times \frac{1}{4} = \frac{8}{4} = 2$ kilometers.
32) **Choice B is correct.** (MA.5.AR.1.3) Dividing a fraction into equal parts is represented by a division expression: $\frac{1}{3} \div 3 = \frac{1}{9}$.
33) **Choice C is correct.** (MA.5.AR.1.3) One yard has 5 fifth-yard pieces. $30 \div \frac{1}{5} = 30 \times 5 = 150$ wristbands.
34) **Choice A is correct.** (MA.5.FR.2.3) Grid: $6 \times 4 = 24$ cells. Shaded (5 of 6 columns, 3 of 4 rows): $5 \times 3 = 15$ cells. Answer: $\frac{15}{24} = \frac{5}{8}$.

35) **The correct answer is 24.** (MA.5.AR.1.3) Each cup contains 4 fourth-cup scoops, so 6 cups contain $6 \times 4 = 24$ scoops.
36) **Choice A is correct.** (MA.5.AR.1.3) The parentheses give $20 - 15 = 5$. Then $100 \div 5 = 20$, and adding 4 gives 24.
37) **Choice A is correct.** (MA.5.AR.2.2) $4200 \div 100 = 42$ cartons. Work backward from the product to find the missing factor.
38) **Choice B is correct.** (MA.5.FR.2.3) Total spent: $4.75 + 2.89 = 7.64$. Remaining: $32.58 - 7.64 = 24.94$ dollars.
39) **Choice A is correct.** (MA.5.NSO.2.3) $V = 10 \times 4 \times 7 = 280$ ft^3.
40) **Choice B is correct.** (MA.5.GR.4.1) Look at the y-coordinates. Point $(6, 4)$ has y-coordinate 4, and point $(3, 8)$ has y-coordinate 8. Since 8 is greater than 4, $(3, 8)$ is farther up from the x-axis.

Practice Test 5 Answers and Explanations

1) **Choice D is correct.** (MA.5.FR.2.3) $\frac{3}{3} = 1$, so $6 \times \frac{3}{3} = 6 \times 1 = 6$.
2) **Choice D is correct.** (MA.5.FR.2.1) LCM(12,4) = 12. $\frac{1}{4} = \frac{3}{12}$. $\frac{7}{12} + \frac{3}{12} = \frac{10}{12} = \frac{5}{6}$ mile.
3) **Choice B is correct.** (MA.5.GR.4.2) Multiplying input by 5 gives output: $2 \times 5 = 10$, $4 \times 5 = 20$, $6 \times 5 = 30$, $8 \times 5 = 40$.
4) **Choice B is correct.** (MA.5.FR.2.1) Common denominator is 15. $\frac{2}{5} = \frac{6}{15}$ and $\frac{1}{3} = \frac{5}{15}$. Since $6 > 5$, $\frac{2}{5} > \frac{1}{3}$.
5) **Choice A is correct.** (MA.5.GR.4.1) The 1st term is 50. To get to the 10th term, subtract 3 nine times: $50 - 27 = 23$.
6) **Choice B is correct.** (MA.5.GR.4.1) The base area is $18 \times 7 = 126$ square centimeters. Since $252 \div 126 = 2$, the height is 2 cm.
7) **Choice B is correct.** (MA.5.AR.2.1) Expression A is the amount $(12 + 8)$. Expression B is 4 copies of that same amount, so B is 4 times as much as A.
8) **Choice A is correct.** (MA.5.GR.3.3) Use the rectangular-prism volume formula: $9 \times 7 \times 7 = 441$. So the volume is 441 cubic centimeters.
9) **The correct answer is 0.45.** (MA.5.NSO.1.1) Multiplying by 10 moves the decimal point one place right: $0.045 \rightarrow 0.45$.
10) **Choice A is correct.** (MA.5.NSO.1.1) Convert 2 km to meters: $2 \times 1000 = 2000$ m. Subtract: $2000 - 1200 = 800$ m.
11) **Choice C is correct.** (MA.5.M.2.1) First cyclist's total: $15.5+8.25 = 23.75$ km. Second cyclist's total: $9.75+12 = 21.75$ km. The first cyclist traveled $23.75 - 21.75 = 2$ km farther.
12) **Choice A is correct.** (MA.5.GR.4.2) The second coordinate is double the first coordinate, then add 3. For $x = 4$, $2(4) + 3 = 11$, so the next point is (4, 11).
13) **Choice B is correct.** (MA.5.NSO.2.2) $840 \div 35 = 24$. Check: $35 \times 24 = 840$.
14) **Choice B is correct.** (MA.5.NSO.2.2) $15 \times 10^7 = 15 \times 10000000 = 150000000$, which is 150 million.
15) **The correct answer is $\frac{5}{9}$.** (MA.5.FR.2.3) Multiplying by 1 does not change the value, so $1 \times \frac{5}{9} = \frac{5}{9}$.
16) **Choice B is correct.** (MA.5.FR.2.3) The parentheses tell us that $6 - 2$ is one grouped amount: "the difference of 6 and 2." Then 8 is multiplied by that difference.
17) **Choice D is correct.** (MA.5.NSO.2.4) The tenths place is 5. The hundredths place is 4. Since $4 < 5$, keep 5. So 12.542 rounds to 12.5.
18) **Choice C is correct.** (MA.5.NSO.2.4) Multiply: $56 \times 15 = 840$, then place decimal two places from right: $8.40 = 8.4$.
19) **Choice B is correct.** (MA.5.FR.2.3) Multiplying by 100 moves the decimal two places right: $2.5 \rightarrow 25 \rightarrow 250$.
20) **Choice B is correct.** (MA.5.FR.2.3) Subtract: $5 - 2\frac{1}{4} = 2\frac{3}{4}$.
21) **Choice C is correct.** (MA.5.FR.2.1) $11\frac{3}{4} - 6\frac{1}{4} = 5\frac{2}{4} = 5\frac{1}{2}$ lb.
22) **Choices B, C, D are correct.** (MA.5.GR.1.2) A square has four right angles, four equal sides, and two pairs of parallel sides.
23) **Choice A is correct.** (MA.5.FR.2.1) $\frac{2}{5} = \frac{4}{10}$. $\frac{4}{10} - \frac{1}{10} = \frac{3}{10}$.
24) **Choice C is correct.** (MA.5.GR.1.1) A rectangle is defined as a quadrilateral with all four angles equal to $90°$. Trapezoids, rhombuses, and general parallelograms do not have this property.
25) **Choice B is correct.** (MA.5.M.1.1) Since 1 pound = 16 ounces, divide 16 by 8: $16 \div 8 = 2$ packages.
26) **Choice C is correct.** (MA.5.AR.2.1) Multiplication is commutative, which means the order of the factors can switch without changing the product. So 9×14 and 14×9 are equal.
27) **Choice C is correct.** (MA.5.GR.3.1) The enlarged prism has dimensions 6 units, 8 units, and 10 units. Its volume is $6 \times 8 \times 10 = 480$ cubic units.

28) **Choice C is correct.** (MA.5.AR.1.3) Start with one unit fraction, $\frac{1}{3}$, and share it into 6 equal parts. Each part is $\frac{1}{3} \div 6 = \frac{1}{18}$ of the whole.
29) **Choice A is correct.** (MA.5.NSO.2.3) Line up decimal points and subtract place by place. $16.83 - 4.58 = 12.25$. This confirms the answer.
30) **The correct answer is** $(4, 20)$. (MA.5.GR.4.2) The 4th term of Pattern A is 4, and the 4th term of Pattern B is 20. So the ordered pair is $(4, 20)$.
31) **The correct answer is 3645.** (MA.5.GR.4.2) $135 \times 7 = 945$ and $135 \times 20 = 2{,}700$. Sum: $945 + 2{,}700 = 3{,}645$.
32) **Choice D is correct.** (MA.5.NSO.2.2) Combine: $42 + 35 = 77$ shaded squares. So $0.42 + 0.35 = 0.77$.
33) **Choice B is correct.** (MA.5.AR.2.2) The parentheses show the size of one group: $(2 + 3)$ units. There are 3 equal groups, so the expression is $3 \times (2 + 3)$.
34) **Choice B is correct.** (MA.5.FR.2.3) $\frac{2}{3} \times 6 = \frac{12}{3} = 4$.
35) **Choice D is correct.** (MA.5.FR.2.3) The four points form the corners of a rectangle with width 8 units (from $x = 1$ to $x = 9$) and height 7 units (from $y = 1$ to $y = 8$).
36) **Choice D is correct.** (MA.5.FR.2.3) Dividing by 10 moves the decimal point one place to the left. $4,300 \div 10 = 430$.
37) **Choice A is correct.** (MA.5.FR.2.3) $2\frac{1}{2} \times 5 = \frac{5}{2} \times 5 = \frac{25}{2} = 12\frac{1}{2}$ dollars.
38) **The correct answer is** $\frac{3}{8}$. (MA.5.GR.2.1) Split into 4 columns and 2 rows = 8 parts; overlap is $3 \times 1 = 3$ parts: $\frac{3}{8}$.
39) **Choice B is correct.** (MA.5.GR.1.1) A right triangle has exactly one right angle (90 degrees) and two other angles that are acute.
40) **Choice D is correct.** (MA.5.AR.1.3) The unit fraction is the amount being shared, so divide $\frac{1}{12}$ by 4. The equation is $\frac{1}{12} \div 4 = n$.

Practice Test 6 Answers and Explanations

1) **Choice C is correct.** (MA.5.GR.4.1) To find the highest point, look for the largest y-coordinate. Point N at $(2, 9)$ has y-coordinate 9, which is the largest.
2) **Choice B is correct.** (MA.5.FR.2.3) $5 \times \frac{1}{2} = 2\frac{1}{2}$. The product is halfway between 0 and 5 because the scaling factor is $\frac{1}{2}$.
3) **Choice B is correct.** (MA.5.AR.1.3) $\frac{1}{8} \div 5 = \frac{1}{8} \times \frac{1}{5} = \frac{1}{40}$.
4) **Choice B is correct.** (MA.5.GR.1.2) The number 3 is in the intersection. A square has four right angles and four equal sides, so it belongs in both circles.
5) **Choice D is correct.** (MA.5.NSO.1.3) Both equal 5 tenths or 50 hundredths. Trailing zeros do not change the decimal's value.
6) **The correct answer is** $\frac{3}{5}$. (MA.5.NSO.1.3) Divide both by 5: $\frac{15 \div 5}{25 \div 5} = \frac{3}{5}$.
7) **Choice D is correct.** (MA.5.FR.2.1) The x-coordinate is 5 (blocks east) and the y-coordinate is 3 (blocks north), so the coordinates are $(5, 3)$.
8) **Choice A is correct.** (MA.5.FR.2.1) Multiples of 12: 12, 24, 36, ... Multiples of 9: 9, 18, 27, 36, ... The first common multiple is 36, so the LCD is 36.
9) **Choice A is correct.** (MA.5.FR.2.1) A is 150 cm, B is 15 cm, C is 1.5 cm. The largest is 150 cm.
10) **Choice B is correct.** (MA.5.GR.1.2) A square has 4 equal sides AND all right angles, making it both a rectangle and a rhombus. Equal sides do not exclude being a rectangle.
11) **Choice C is correct.** (MA.5.DP.1.1) Lowest: 15°C (1 mark), Highest: 24°C (4 marks). Difference: $24 - 15 = 9$°C.
12) **Choice B is correct.** (MA.5.AR.1.1) Scale factor: $80 \div 20 = 4$. Sugar needed: $1.25 \times 4 = 5.00$ kilograms.
13) **Choice A is correct.** (MA.5.NSO.1.2) In 2.04, the 0 holds the tenths place and the 4 is in the hundredths place. So the correct reading is "two and four hundredths."
14) **The correct answer is** $\frac{7}{12}$. (MA.5.FR.2.3) Multiply across to get $\frac{14}{24}$. Both numbers are divisible by 2, so $\frac{14}{24} = \frac{7}{12}$.
15) **Choice D is correct.** (MA.5.FR.2.3) The x-coordinate represents units right from the origin: 9 units. The y-coordinate represents units up: 4 units. So the coordinates are $(9, 4)$.
16) **Choice B is correct.** (MA.5.FR.2.3) The diagram shows $73.5 \div 10 = 7.35$ grams. Dividing by 10 moves decimal 1 place left.
17) **Choice C is correct.** (MA.5.AR.1.2) Convert: $\frac{1}{5} = \frac{2}{10}$. Total: $\frac{2}{10} + \frac{2}{10} = \frac{4}{10} = \frac{2}{5}$ of the inventory sold.

18) **Choices A, B are correct.** (MA.5.GR.2.1) C is addition; D equals $\frac{3}{4}$, not $\frac{3}{8}$.
19) **Choice B is correct.** (MA.5.GR.3.1) The known length and height make groups of $18 \times 8 = 144$ cubic inches. Since $432 \div 144 = 3$, the width is 3 inches.
20) **Choice A is correct.** (MA.5.GR.3.1) $V = 13 \times 2 \times 4 = 104$ m^3.
21) **Choice C is correct.** (MA.5.GR.3.1) The prism is only 1 unit tall, so it has one layer. The layer has $7 \times 2 = 14$ unit cubes.
22) **Choice A is correct.** (MA.5.AR.1.2) $\frac{1}{3} \times 30 = \frac{30}{3} = 10$.
23) **Choice D is correct.** (MA.5.FR.2.1) LCM(5,10) = 10. $\frac{2}{5} = \frac{4}{10}$. $\frac{4}{10} + \frac{3}{10} = \frac{7}{10}$ yard.
24) **Choice B is correct.** (MA.5.GR.4.2) Compare each pair: $1 \times 7 = 7$, $2 \times 7 = 14$, $3 \times 7 = 21$, and $4 \times 7 = 28$.
25) **Choice D is correct.** (MA.5.AR.2.2) Simplify both groups first: $9 - 3 = 6$ and $4 + 2 = 6$. Then work left to right: $6 \times 6 = 36$, and $36 \div 4 = 9$.
26) **Choice C is correct.** (MA.5.AR.2.2) $14 \div \frac{1}{3} = 14 \times 3 = 42$.
27) **Choice A is correct.** (MA.5.AR.1.3) In expanded form, $7.346 = 7 + 0.3$ (tenths) $+ 0.04$ (hundredths) $+ 0.006$ (thousandths).
28) **Choice C is correct.** (MA.5.NSO.2.2) Multiply: $225 \times 4 = (200 \times 4) + (20 \times 4) + (5 \times 4) = 800 + 80 + 20 = 900$.
29) **The correct answer is 132 cm^3.** (MA.5.NSO.2.2) The expression multiplies each prism's three dimensions, then adds the volumes. The values are 72 and 60, for a total of 132 cubic centimeters. Accept any equivalent expression that finds both prism volumes and adds them, and accept the numeric answer 132 cm^3.
30) **Choice D is correct.** (MA.5.GR.4.2) At step 4, W = 12 and X = 4. The sum is $12 + 4 = 16$.
31) **Choice D is correct.** (MA.5.DP.1.1) Count X marks at 4, 5, and 6. That is $3 + 4 + 1 = 8$ students who read at least 4 books.
32) **Choice D is correct.** (MA.5.FR.2.2) $9\frac{2}{3} \approx 10$ and $6\frac{8}{9} \approx 7$. So $9\frac{2}{3} - 6\frac{8}{9} \approx 10 - 7 = 3$.
33) **Choice B is correct.** (MA.5.FR.2.2) $5 \times 1000 = 5000$. Append three zeros to 5.
34) **Choice D is correct.** (MA.5.AR.1.3) $2 \div \frac{1}{6} = 2 \times 6 = 12$ lessons.
35) **Choice D is correct.** (MA.5.AR.1.3) Since $40 \times 50 = 2{,}000$ and $2{,}000 \div 10 = 200$, there are 200 groups of 10 in the product.
36) **Choice A is correct.** (MA.5.FR.2.3) A power of 10 tells how many factors of 10 to use. In order: 100, 300, 2000, 10000. This confirms the answer.
37) **Choice A is correct.** (MA.5.NSO.2.2) $1,232 \div 16 = 77$ pounds per animal. Check: $16 \times 77 = 1,232$.
38) **The correct answer is 2.** (MA.5.GR.3.1) $30 \div (5 \times 3) = 30 \div 15 = 2$.
39) **The correct answer is 72 cubic feet.** (MA.5.GR.3.1) The garden bed is a rectangular prism, so multiply the three dimensions: $9 \times 4 \times 2 = 72$ cubic feet.
40) **Choice D is correct.** (MA.5.GR.3.3) LCD = 15. $\frac{3}{5} = \frac{9}{15}$; $\frac{2}{3} = \frac{10}{15}$. $\frac{10}{15} - \frac{9}{15} = \frac{1}{15}$.

Practice Test 7 Answers and Explanations

1) **Choice B is correct.** (MA.5.AR.2.1) Both expressions have the same factor, 4.2. Since 5 is less than 5.1, the product with 5 is smaller.
2) **The correct answer is 12.** (MA.5.AR.2.1) Convert meters to centimeters before dividing. Since 3 m is 300 cm and each piece is 25 cm, $300 \div 25 = 12$ pieces.
3) **Choice A is correct.** (MA.5.M.2.1) Since 1 gallon = 16 cups, multiply 2 by 16: $2 \times 16 = 32$ cups.
4) **Choice B is correct.** (MA.5.M.1.1) Add: $2\frac{1}{6} + 4\frac{5}{6} = 6\frac{6}{6} = 7$.
5) **Choice B is correct.** (MA.5.FR.2.1) Check: for first coordinates 1, 2, and 3, doubling and adding 1 gives 3, 5, and 7.
6) **Choice A is correct.** (MA.5.FR.2.3) 0.6×4 means four groups of 0.6. Option A shows 0.6 four times, which is 2.4 in all.
7) **The correct answer is 7.5 m.** (MA.5.M.1.1) $750 \div 100 = 7.5$ m. Since 100 centimeters make 1 meter, divide centimeters by 100.
8) **Choice D is correct.** (MA.5.M.1.1) The amount being scaled is the sum $(10 + 7)$. The phrase "3 times as many as" means multiply that whole sum by 3.
9) **Choice D is correct.** (MA.5.GR.3.3) The base area is $10 \times 6 = 60$ square feet. Since $360 \div 60 = 6$, the locker is 6 ft tall.

10) **Choice B is correct.** (MA.5.GR.4.1) Rule: Output $= 7\times$ Input; $7 \times 4 = 28$.

11) **Choice D is correct.** (MA.5.NSO.2.4) 2.48 is 0.08 away from 2.4 and only 0.02 away from 2.5, so it is closer to 2.5. When rounded to the nearest tenth, 2.48 rounds to 2.5.

12) **Choice D is correct.** (MA.5.FR.2.1) $\frac{5}{16}$ is not equivalent to $\frac{1}{3}$ because $1 \times 16 \neq 3 \times 5$. The other choices simplify to $\frac{1}{3}$.

13) **Choice C is correct.** (MA.5.FR.2.3) $\frac{1}{4} \times \frac{1}{5} = \frac{1}{20}$ (multiply numerators and denominators).

14) **Choice D is correct.** (MA.5.AR.1.3) Each whole contains 3 pieces of size $\frac{1}{3}$. With 3 wholes, there are $3 \times 3 = 9$ pieces.

15) **The correct answer is $3\frac{5}{8}$.** (MA.5.FR.2.1) $6\frac{1}{4} = 6\frac{2}{8} = 5\frac{10}{8}$. Subtract: $(5-2) + (\frac{10}{8} - \frac{5}{8}) = 3\frac{5}{8}$.

16) **Choice D is correct.** (MA.5.FR.2.1) The student found the base area $(9 \times 5 = 45)$ but forgot to multiply by height. The correct volume is $9 \times 5 \times 4 = 180$ cm^3.

17) **Choice A is correct.** (MA.5.GR.2.1) The overlap has $3 \times 4 = 12$ squares out of 60 total, so the fraction is $\frac{12}{60} = \frac{1}{5}$.

18) **Choices A, C are correct.** (MA.5.AR.2.1) B and D do not group $5 + 2$ before multiplying.

19) **Choice C is correct.** (MA.5.FR.2.3) $30 \times \frac{3}{5} = 18$ marbles. Since $\frac{3}{5} < 1$, the result is smaller than 30.

20) **Choice D is correct.** (MA.5.GR.3.2) Find each part first: Prism A is $7 \times 4 \times 2 = 56$ cubic meters, and Prism B is $6 \times 2 \times 1 = 12$ cubic meters. Because the parts do not overlap, add them: $56 + 12 = 68$ cubic meters.

21) **Choice D is correct.** (MA.5.AR.1.3) $\frac{1}{2} \div 4 = \frac{1}{2} \times \frac{1}{4} = \frac{1}{8}$ cup.

22) **Choice D is correct.** (MA.5.FR.2.1) Listing multiples helps you find the smallest number both denominators divide into evenly. That smallest shared multiple is the least common denominator.

23) **Choice C is correct.** (MA.5.DP.1.1) Count the X marks at each height on the line plot. The height with the greatest number of X marks is 5 inches, which has 4 plants. Therefore, the most common plant height is 5 inches.

24) **Choice B is correct.** (MA.5.FR.2.2) A is close to $\frac{1}{2}$, B equals $\frac{1}{2}$, C is about 0.4, and D is about 0.41. B is exact, so it is the closest.

25) **Choice D is correct.** (MA.5.GR.1.2) The squares are also rectangles, so the total number of rectangles is $6 + 4 = 10$.

26) **Choice B is correct.** (MA.5.FR.2.3) $0.023 \times 100 = 2.3$ (move decimal 2 places right).

27) **Choice B is correct.** (MA.5.FR.2.3) Point T is 2 units to the right and 8 units up from the origin, so it is at $(2, 8)$.

28) **Choice B is correct.** (MA.5.GR.4.2) Each F value is 3 times the matching E value: $2 \times 3 = 6$, $4 \times 3 = 12$, $6 \times 3 = 18$, and $8 \times 3 = 24$.

29) **Choice A is correct.** (MA.5.AR.1.2) Area $= \frac{7}{8} \times \frac{3}{5} = \frac{21}{40}$ m^2.

30) **Choice D is correct.** (MA.5.AR.1.3) $2 \div \frac{1}{3} = 2 \times 3 = 6$. There are 6 one-third pizzas in 2 whole pizzas.

31) **Choice C is correct.** (MA.5.FR.2.3) Any positive number multiplied by a factor less than 1 always produces a smaller result.

32) **The correct answer is 3 sides.** (MA.5.GR.1.1) An equilateral triangle has 3 equal sides and 3 vertices. A square has 4 sides and 4 vertices, so the number of sides or vertices tells the shapes apart.

33) **Choice C is correct.** (MA.5.AR.1.1) Multiply the price per pound by the number of pounds: $0.85 \times 6.5 = 5.525$ dollars. Money is written to the nearest cent, so this rounds to \$5.53.

34) **The correct answer is 70.** (MA.5.FR.2.3) Multiplying by 1,000 moves the decimal point three places right: $0.07 \to 70$.

35) **Choice A is correct.** (MA.5.FR.2.3) $\frac{6}{10}$ has denominator 10, so the digit 6 goes in the tenths place: 0.6. Sarah incorrectly wrote 0.06, which represents $\frac{6}{100}$.

36) **Choice B is correct.** (MA.5.FR.2.3) Five copies of $\frac{1}{6}$ make $\frac{5}{6}$. The denominator stays 6 because the size of each piece is still sixths.

37) **Choice D is correct.** (MA.5.FR.2.3) $10^3 = 1{,}000$, so $6{,}800 \div 1{,}000 = 6.8$.

38) **Choice A is correct.** (MA.5.FR.2.3) This is a count of half-pound groups in 1 pound: $1 \div \frac{1}{2} = 2$ groups.

39) **Choice D is correct.** (MA.5.FR.2.3) Convert to an improper fraction: $2\frac{1}{3} = \frac{7}{3}$. Multiply: $\frac{7}{3} \times 3 = \frac{7\times 3}{3} = 7$.

40) **Choice C is correct.** (MA.5.FR.2.3) Division comes before addition and subtraction, so $8 \div 2 = 4$. Now finish left to right: $9 + 4 - 3 = 10$.

Practice Test 8 Answers and Explanations

1) **Choice B is correct.** (MA.5.GR.4.2) Using the rule $\times 2 + 3$: when input is 5, output $= 5 \times 2 + 3 = 13$.

2) **Choice D is correct.** (MA.5.GR.1.1) One 90-degree angle = right; all different sides = scalene. Combined: right scalene.
3) **The correct answer is 6.** (MA.5.GR.3.3) The known length and height make groups of $6 \times 4 = 24$ cubic centimeters. Since $144 \div 24 = 6$, the width is 6 cm.
4) **Choice B is correct.** (MA.5.GR.3.3) "The sum of 12 and 8" means group $12 + 8$. "Half of" that sum means divide the grouped total by 2.
5) **Choice C is correct.** (MA.5.GR.1.1) A pentagon has 5 sides, while a quadrilateral has 4 sides. So a pentagon is not a quadrilateral.
6) **Choice A is correct.** (MA.5.GR.3.1) $V = B \times h = 28 \times 11 = 308$ ft^3.
7) **The correct answer is 0.067.** (MA.5.GR.3.1) Move the decimal point two places left, adding a zero as a placeholder: $6.7 \rightarrow 0.067$.
8) **Choice C is correct.** (MA.5.FR.2.3) Both points have the same x-coordinate (3), so the distance is $9 - 4 = 5$ miles north.
9) **Choice C is correct.** (MA.5.GR.1.2) A parallelogram with all sides equal is a rhombus. This is the most specific classification.
10) **Choice B is correct.** (MA.5.GR.1.2) Option B ($5.82 - 2.56$) requires borrowing because 2 hundredths is not enough to subtract 6 hundredths. Borrow 1 tenth to make 12 hundredths.
11) **Choice C is correct.** (MA.5.FR.2.1) LCM(6,4) = 12. $\frac{5}{6} = \frac{10}{12}$ and $\frac{3}{4} = \frac{9}{12}$. $\frac{10}{12} + \frac{9}{12} = \frac{19}{12} = 1\frac{7}{12}$.
12) **Choice D is correct.** (MA.5.FR.2.3) Multiplying 3.2 by 100 moves the decimal two places right, giving 320.
13) **Choice C is correct.** (MA.5.FR.2.3) Add the ribbon lengths shown by the marks: $(1 \times 3) + (3 \times 2) + (5 \times 3) + (7 \times 1) = 31$ inches. Sharing 31 inches equally among 4 posters gives $31 \div 4 = 7\frac{3}{4}$ inches per poster.
14) **Choice C is correct.** (MA.5.FR.2.3) Both equal 5000: $50 \times 100 = 5000$ and $500 \times 10 = 5000$.
15) **Choice C is correct.** (MA.5.M.2.1) Number of sections: $72 \div 8 = 9$. Posts needed: $9 + 1 = 10$ (one at each end and one at each division between sections).
16) **Choice C is correct.** (MA.5.GR.3.1) Base area $= 25 \times 5 = 125$ cm^2. Height $= 500 \div 125 = 4$ cm.
17) **Choice B is correct.** (MA.5.GR.3.1) $2 \times 4 \times 3 = 24$ cubic units. Choice A: $2 \times 3 \times 3 = 18$. Choice C: $2 \times 2 \times 5 = 20$. Choice D: $3 \times 3 \times 2 = 18$.
18) **Choice B is correct.** (MA.5.FR.2.3) The nonzero parts make $6 \times 7 = 42$, which has no trailing zero. The three factor zeros give 42,000, so there are 3 zeros.
19) **Choices A, B are correct.** (MA.5.AR.1.2) $2\frac{1}{3} - 1\frac{1}{2} = \frac{5}{6}$ cup left, so A is true. Since $\frac{5}{6}$ is less than 1, B is also true. C miscomputes; D is false.
20) **Choice B is correct.** (MA.5.NSO.2.2) Round 511 to 500. Then $500 \times 9 = 4,500$.
21) **The correct answer is 40.** (MA.5.NSO.2.2) Multiply length, width, and height to count the unit cubes. $2 \times 4 \times 5 = 40$ cubic units.
22) **Choice B is correct.** (MA.5.GR.3.1) Point B is at 0.525, which is 0.025 from 0.5. Point A (0.205) is 0.295 away, and C (0.75) is 0.25 away. Point B is closest.
23) **Choice D is correct.** (MA.5.GR.4.2) Use output = input × input. With input 5, the output is $5 \times 5 = 25$, so the ordered pair is $(5, 25)$.
24) **Choice B is correct.** (MA.5.AR.2.2) Move outward through the grouping symbols: $5 - 2 = 3$, then $[4 \times 3] = 12$, then $\{3 + 12\} = 15$. Finally, $2 \times 15 = 30$.
25) **Choice B is correct.** (MA.5.NSO.1.1) The number is 9.428. In expanded form: $9 + 0.4 + 0.02 + 0.008$.
26) **Choice A is correct.** (MA.5.NSO.2.3) Subtract: $5.72 - 2.45 = 3.27$. Check: $2.45 + 3.27 = 5.72$.
27) **Choice C is correct.** (MA.5.NSO.2.3) Convert 1.2 L to mL: $1.2 \times 1000 = 1200$ mL. Both containers hold 1,200 mL.
28) **The correct answer is 10000.** (MA.5.FR.2.3) 10^4 means $10 \times 10 \times 10 \times 10 = 10{,}000$ (a 1 followed by 4 zeros).
29) **Choice C is correct.** (MA.5.FR.2.3) Use the rectangular-prism volume formula: $8 \times 5 \times 5 = 200$. So the volume is 200 cubic feet.
30) **Choice D is correct.** (MA.5.AR.1.3) The model counts sixths inside 3 wholes. So the matching equation is $3 \div \frac{1}{6} = n$.
31) **Choice D is correct.** (MA.5.FR.2.1) Borrow 1 from 7: $6\frac{12}{10} - 3\frac{7}{10} = 3\frac{5}{10}$. Simplify $\frac{5}{10}$ to $\frac{1}{2}$, so the difference is $3\frac{1}{2}$.
32) **Choice B is correct.** (MA.5.AR.2.1) The scaled bars show the relative sizes of the expressions. The longest bar is labeled $5 \times (6 + 8)$, so that expression has the greatest value.
33) **Choice B is correct.** (MA.5.FR.2.1) Add whole parts: $4 + 2 = 6$. Add fractions: $\frac{3}{8} + \frac{1}{8} = \frac{4}{8} = \frac{1}{2}$. Result: $6\frac{1}{2}$.
34) **The correct answer is 4.** (MA.5.GR.4.2) Each Y value is 4 times the matching X value: $4 \div 1 = 4$, $8 \div 2 = 4$, and so on.

35) **Choice D is correct.** (MA.5.GR.4.2) $567 \div 21 = 27$. Check: $21 \times 27 = 567$.

36) **Choice C is correct.** (MA.5.NSO.2.2) $3.6 \times 4 = 14.4$. Following the pattern, each time the multiplier doubles, the product doubles.

37) **Choice C is correct.** (MA.5.M.1.1) First add the liquid amounts: $1\frac{1}{2} + \frac{1}{2} = 2$ cups. Since 1 cup is 8 fl oz, $2 \times 8 = 16$ fl oz.

38) **Choice B is correct.** (MA.5.NSO.2.4) The hundredths place is 7. The thousandths place is 8. Since $8 \geq 5$, round up from 7 to 8. So 5.678 rounds to 5.68.

39) **Choice D is correct.** (MA.5.NSO.2.4) Pattern A adds 1 each time and Pattern B adds 3 each time. The next matching values are 5 and 15, so the next ordered pair is $(5, 15)$.

40) **Choice B is correct.** (MA.5.FR.2.1) $\frac{9}{10} - \frac{3}{10} = \frac{6}{10}$.

Testinar Grade 5 Online Center

So Much More Online! *Discover amazing resources to help you succeed!*

Testinar Math Grade 5 Online Center offers a complete study program, including:

- ✓ All the tools you need to master Grade 5 math concepts
- ✓ Printable practice sets that sharpen daily problem-solving
- ✓ Free full-length Grade 5 math practice tests to track progress
- ✓ Study guides and pacing tips that fit real classroom schedules
- ✓ And much more . . .

Scan Me

No Registration Required! Start learning right away—it's completely free and easy! **Visit Testinar.com/Grade5** *You've got this! Keep learning and growing!*

Notes From Your Math Architect

Dear Builder of Big Ideas,

◇ Across 8 practice tests, you laid down brick after brick of math skill. The foundation is solid. The walls are strong. The roof is in place. You've built yourself a study sturdy enough to stand any storm test day might bring. ◇

⋆ **What architects know:** a great building starts with a great plan. You've practiced planning—reading carefully, picking your strategy, and working step by step. That blueprint thinking is what turns hard problems into clear answers. ⋆

Builder's Inspection Checklist

- **Foundation:** ROCK SOLID! Number sense, fractions, decimals—all in place.
- **Frame:** STRONG! You can break down a problem into clear parts.
- **Walls:** TIGHT! Your work is organized and easy to follow.
- **Roof:** FINISHED! You always answer the question that was asked.

Architect's tip: on test day, build each answer like a small building. Foundation: read the question. Frame: pick the strategy. Walls: do the math. Roof: check the answer. Each piece matters. Each piece is yours.

If you'd like to share your experience or have questions, please email me at reza@testinar.com. I'd love to hear from you!

Reza Nazari & Jay Daie

Your Math Architect (Built to Last)

www.ingramcontent.com/pod-product-compliance
Lightning Source LLC
LaVergne TN
LVHW060038210926
848481LV00013B/3897